How Intelligence Happens

John Duncan

How
Intelligence
Happens

Yale UNIVERSITY PRESS

NEW HAVEN AND LONDON

Published with assistance from the Louis Stern Memorial Fund.

Yale University Press books may be purchased in quantity for educational, business, or promotional use. For information, please e-mail sales.press@ yale.edu (U.S. office) or sales@yaleup.co.uk (U.K. office).

Designed by Nancy Ovedovitz and set in Monotype Joanna type by Duke & Company, Devon, Pennsylvania. Printed in the United States of America by The Maple Press Company, York, PA.

Library of Congress Cataloging-in-Publication Data
Duncan, John.
How intelligence happens / John Duncan.
    p. cm.
Includes bibliographical references and index.
ISBN 978-0-300-15411-5 (clothbound : alk. paper) 1. Intellect. 2. Brain.
3. Thought and thinking. 4. Neurobiology. I. Title.
BF431.D86 2010
153—dc22   2010013170

A catalogue record for this book is available from the British Library.
This paper meets the requirements of ANSI/NISO Z39.48–1992
(Permanence of Paper).

10 9 8 7 6 5 4 3 2 1

To
my mother
for the soup and bread

and my wife
for the sense of adventure

Contents

Acknowledgments

To all those people who read earlier versions of this book, I am grateful for both encouragements and improvements: Phil Barnard, Nancy Kanwisher, Earl Miller, Richard Partridge, Mike Posner, Jane Raymond, Valia Rodriguez, Steffen Stoewer, Mark Stokes, Mitch Valdes-Sosa, Rob Ward, a variety of Duncans and Eldridges, my agent, Peter Tallack, and above all my editor, Jean Thomson Black. The text flowed a good deal better after the expert polish applied by my manuscript editor, Laura Jones Dooley, and for many of the figures I had only pretty rough ideas; Russell Thompson and Simon Strangeways did the rest. Of course, my greatest debt is to the many people who have helped over the years with my education, especially Pat Rabbitt, Mike Posner, Tim Shallice, Bob Desimone, and David Gaffan.

Prologue The Cows in the River and the
View toward the Malecón

t is a midsummer's afternoon; with my brother and sister I lie on
the riverbank, too idle to relaunch our raft, watching the flicking
and splashing of a small group of my father's cows at the water's
edge. They, too, are dazed by the heat; over the water are clouds of
dragonflies; there is the smell of cows, the river, hot summer grass.
Perhaps I am nursing my bare foot; this field has thistles.

The cows have come to the water to drink. Now they stand cool-
ing in the current, ears and tails flicking at flies. One looks up to
watch the children at the riverside, considers for a moment, and then
returns to drinking. One rears up on to the back of another, a signal
that the one beneath is ready for the bull, and there is a staggering
and splashing before the two break apart. One is perhaps disturbed or
perhaps no longer hot; she raises her head from the water, squelches
to shore, and, gaining the top of the riverbank, dips her head to the
grass to eat.

Now I am older. Outside my Havana hotel, I am leaning again in
the sun, awaiting my ride to work. Here the sun is hotter. In front is
an open area where streets meet, with a small park behind and then

the blue of the inlet that gives access to the harbor. In the park, a tuft of banana trees; in front, a wide strip of shade where the little cycle taxis park; behind and to the right, busy streets with Cuba's darting children, patched cars, everywhere people on foot; ahead to the left, the road sweeps away and out of sight toward the long waterfront curve of the Malecón.

Everybody is going about their business. In the shade by the park, a man in cutoffs is reaching into the canopy of his bicycle taxi, fiddling with the straps. In the center of the open space stand two police-men, stern but very young in their uniforms. The two are vigilant for traffic infractions; suddenly one raises his whistle and blows as an ancient car emerges rapidly the wrong way from the mouth of a one-way street. A mother ushers her sparkling-clean children along the pavement. On the inlet, a small boat putters by; inside it two men are reorganizing their fishing tackle.

My colleague has a Cuban's adaptability. Sometimes she turns up in her car; sometimes her battery has died and she has persuaded a friend to bring her (this is not easy; fuel is hard to come by); once she arrives in an official vehicle from the Neuroscience Center. In Cuba it is easy to have one's goals overturned, but nothing stops my colleague; no matter what, she always turns up on time.

The great adventure of science is the search for general organi-zational principles, principles that can bring order to an apparently bewildering chaos of natural phenomena. Our universe is a tumult of moving objects—trees blowing in the wind, planets traversing the sky, an avalanche demolishing a mountainside, a dragonfly hovering above a pond. In Newton's laws of motion, simple principles reduce this chaos to order, allowing a schoolchild to calculate when, how, and how much a body will move as forces act on it. New discoveries bring new phenomena to be explained—exchange between energy and mass, the origins and expansion of the universe. With Einstein and the progress of modern physics, explanatory principles become ever more general and powerful. Our world teems with an apparently infinite diversity of plant and animal life, populated with every variety of color, form, habitat, growth. In Darwin's theory of evolution, this infinite variety is linked, structured, and made comprehensible.

Perhaps few phenomena seem so diverse and chaotic as animal behavior—the circling of a hawk followed by the stoop on its prey; the buzz of a fly repeatedly knocking against a window; the opening and closing of sea anemones on a reef and the parrotfish moving among them. As a teenager, I was captivated by the work of the great ethologists Konrad Lorenz and Niko Tinbergen and by the beautiful idea that, through simple principles, the chaos of much animal behavior could also be reduced to order.[1]

In the world of the ethologists, the basic principle of instinctive behavior is the "innate releasing mechanism," or IRM. The IRM detects the presence of some stimulus in the sensory environment, and when this critical stimulus or releaser is detected, a stable pattern of activity is produced. The pattern of activity can be quite complex, but with important, unchanging features; ethologists call it a "fixed action pattern." Each IRM produces a fragment of the species-specific behavior that the animal needs to survive. Concatenated, sequences of IRMs produce behavior of infinite form, variety, and complexity.

The fragments themselves are fascinating, coming from every part of the animal kingdom, involving releasers from every sensory modality and behavior of all kinds.[2] For herring gulls, a speckled object outside the nest releases an organized attempt to roll this object back into the nest for incubation. The object does not need to be rounded, and to a surprising degree, the bigger it is, the more strongly the behavior is released; it is the speckling that is most important, and the gull will struggle with an artificial speckled egg far too large to be its own. A very different behavior is released by an egg with a hole surrounded by a white, serrated edge; this broken egg may attract predators, and its serrated edge releases its removal from the nest. A male stickleback defending its territory attacks approaching objects with a red underside, resembling rival males. Many birds flee from the round, staring eyes of predators such as owls, and some species of moths, touched on their backs, suddenly flash their underwings into view to reveal this same staring eye pattern. A female cricket turns toward the song of a male and moves in its direction; a male moth flies toward the scent released by the female; a human adult senses the need to protect an infant with large eyes and a high forehead.

By combining innate releasing mechanisms or IRMs, elaborate sequences of behavior can be built up. A simple example is a toad preying on a worm.[3] A strong releaser for a toad is an elongated object moving along the direction of its axis. When the toad sees this object to one side, the first IRM produces a turn in its direction. Once the object is straight ahead, a second IRM is triggered, and the toad begins to move forward. Forward movement stops when the object comes within reach; now the toad fixes its head and snaps. Put together, this sequence of IRMs has produced an entire, complex activity, a program of behavior allowing the hungry toad to feed.

In more complex examples, the programs of two or more animals may be coordinated. At the start of the mating season, the male stickleback turns red, stakes out a territory, and builds a nest consisting of a hole covered with weeds. The stage is set for a complex mating sequence, driven by a concatenated series of male and female IRMs.[4] The first male IRM is triggered by the sight of a female stickleback, with swollen belly and a specific, posturing movement, entering the territory. The male approaches and begins a characteristic zigzag dance. Now the first IRM of the female comes into play; seeing the zigzag, she approaches the male. Her approach drives the next male

IRM—he turns and swims rapidly toward the nest; seeing him turn, the female is enticed to follow. As the female is seen to approach the nest, the male responds by pointing his head to the opening; the female responds by entering. At the sight of the female in the nest, the male begins to stimulate spawning; he repeatedly thrusts his head at her rump, and in response, the eggs are laid. Finally, the male detects fresh eggs in the nest and, in response, releases his sperm. Each step in this sequence is somewhat separate from the others; it is the approach of the female to the nest that releases the male's head point; it is the head point that releases the female's entry. The separate IRMs form the elements of the fishes' behavior; in combination, they create a complex whole.

Lorenz maintained that science emerges from fascination, from a simple desire to watch. It is the endless hours of delighted observation that finally bring order from chaos. Through the ideas of the IRM, the releaser, and the fixed action pattern, the early ethologists produced a new description of much animal behavior, and now, seeing through their eyes, we can share this experience. As we watch bees humming in the flowers, seagulls squabbling over scraps, or clouds of fish over a reef, the chaos of our first, casual impression is replaced by the new ethologists' vision. Now we see stable structures of behavior elicited by consistent sensory events, and complex, ever-changing wholes built up through assembly of these fixed, constantly recurring fragments.

Powerful though these ideas are, they cover only a part of animal behavior. The idea of a "fixed action pattern" applies well to the most instinctive behaviors, to patterns that are useful in general to animals of this species and might plausibly have been stamped into the nervous system by evolution. When some signal indicates a cow's sexual receptivity, the IRM provides a good explanation for the mounting that is released in other cows and for the approach of the bull that this mounting in turn releases. For animals in general and humans in particular, the IRM provides a less useful explanation as behavior becomes increasingly flexible and dependent on experience. Cows will drink from the river, from a bucket, from a trough in the farmyard; when they are finished they will go to the stall, where they have learned that the farmer leaves hay. The IRM is of little help in explaining behavior of this sort, and it is no help at all in the behavior of the Cubans in their plaza—in the decision of the mother to clean and dress her children, in the taxi driver who repairs his canopy, in the men who complete their fishing and turn their boat for home. As we watch these people, there is certainly a sense of order. This is not the order, though, of the releaser, the fixed action pattern, and the IRM.

When we turn to the complexity of human thought and behavior, we face one of the great scientific puzzles. Again there is an appearance of infinite variety, of people who construct elaborate meals, write novels, travel in submarines and aircraft, conceive the equations of general relativity. Our own minds, our own intelligence seem incomprehensible in the richness, variety, and power of the thought and behavior they produce. What kind of principles can we use here to impose order on chaos? What equivalent to the IRM can explain the mother scrubbing her children and the fisherman steering his boat?

In this book, I will tell an adventure story—the story of a search for basic principles of human behavior, thought, and intelligence. The adventure takes us to many places. A first clue comes from the classical field of "intelligence testing," beginning more than a century ago with the origins of systematic experimental psychology. The science of intelligence testing has often been lost in political controversy, but from the science comes a significant lead. Simple, apparently trivial psychological tests, looking much like children's puzzles, are related to success in many other activities, from laboratory tasks to achievements in education and at work (chapter 2). How can such tests work? What do they tell us, not just of differences between one person and another, but of human minds in general? To answer the question, the story turns to neuropsychology and the bizarre changes in thought and behavior that can follow brain damage. With damage to specific parts of the cerebral cortex, the mental programs of thought and behavior are derailed. Behavior becomes disorganized, fragmented, ineffective, and with modern methods of brain imaging, we can define the exact brain system that is responsible. We now know that this system plays a role in organizing all that we do, from understanding and remembering a story to planning a trip to the beach or pressing a simple key in response to a picture on a computer screen. It is also at the heart of classical "intelligence" tests and their component psychological functions (chapter 4).

Modern brain imaging tells us *where* this system is found in the brain—but what does it *do*? For the next step, the story turns to intelligent computers and what it takes to create useful, "intelligent" mental programs (chapter 5) solving problems from a proof in symbolic logic to the plan for a day's errands. The work shows something fundamental in intelligence. In general, complex problems can be solved only by decomposition, by finding a useful division into separate, independently solved subproblems. Can brains create these separate cognitive enclosures and assemble them into the organized structures of thought? To answer this question, the story moves on to microelectrode recordings from single cells in the brain's frontal lobes and the remarkable properties that experiments of this sort are just beginning to uncover (chapter 6). Chapter 7 returns to experimental psychology and to a complementary argument. Essential though it is to the power of our minds, the construction of cognitive enclosures also illuminates our most human weaknesses, as competing thoughts vie for access to the mental program and reason degenerates into rationalization.

This is a story of discovery, and certainly it is far from over. It has parts that are strong, parts that are uncertain, and some parts that are no more than a first, outline sketch. Even so, as the parts begin to come together, again we see that a picture is forming. Once more, order begins to emerge from chaos.

Chapter 1 **The Machine**

Thirty years ago, I took a train to Heathrow. I was meeting a good friend, one of many I had made in two years of postdoctoral work at the University of Oregon. This was his first visit to Britain. On the ride back from the airport, looking out over the manicured hedges and fields of the English countryside, he said with wonder, "Oh man, what a conquered country." Very occasionally, flying over Siberia or Greenland, I have looked down on a country that seemed largely unconquered. Otherwise, though, our environment is shaped and filled by the products of the human mind.

For example, looking up from my work here I see . . . a desk, a computer, sheets of paper . . . a window, with a house ahead, a gravel drive to the left, a road beyond with passing motor vehicles . . . beyond that, more houses, television antennas, electricity lines. To the right are gardens, but little in those gardens grew there on its own . . . these plants grew because a person wanted them, dug the earth to plant them, fed them fertilizer, pulled up weeds. In among the plants are fences, sheds, washing lines . . . steam rises from boiler outlets . . . planes pass overhead in the sky. It would be nice to believe that eager readers have taken my book with them to the ice fields of

Antarctica, but more likely, the environment that you will see, raising your eyes from the page, will be just as conquered as mine.

No wonder we find our own minds so fascinating. They give us our human world, with its greatest achievements: medicine, art, food production, shelter, and warmth, all products of the human mind and the power it gives us to transform our existence. They give us also many of the greatest hazards we and our planet face: climate change, the destructions of war, enormous imbalances in the distribution of food and other goods, pollution and ecosystem destruction, pandemics brought on by our own behavior—all products of human choice and action, all avoidable if our minds did not function as they do.

Every organism has its own ecological niche and the special features that have allowed it to survive and flourish. Just as the cheetah runs and the caterpillar sits motionless along the blade of a leaf, so we have our unique intelligence: the intelligence that created the desk, the window, the passing cars and planes. We love to watch this intelligence at work, as a child first fits together the pieces of a jigsaw or recites her first nursery rhyme, as a student stares intently at the calculus teacher and suddenly, from nowhere, there is a fizz of understanding and shared delight. We admire human intelligence in architecture, in well-oiled machinery, in an argument perfectly constructed. This is what we are, and this is why so much of our world is now so firmly in our hands.

But how? Surely, the nature of human intelligence is among the most challenging, the most fascinating, and—both for ourselves and for our planet—the most essentially important of questions. How should we understand the human mind and the human behavior that so powerfully shapes our world?

One approach to understanding human minds is thoroughly familiar. It is how we grew up, how we operate many times each day, how we manage our affairs. Essentially, it is the explanation of human choice and action through reason. We see ourselves as rational agents. Our choices have reasons, and when we describe those reasons, we explain the things that we chose to do.

This perspective is evident in all that we do. History's explanations are accounts of what people wanted, what they knew or believed, what they intended to achieve. As the Russians retreated before Napoleon, they burned crops because they intended the French army to starve. John F. Kennedy held back from a strike on Cuba because he believed that such a strike could force the Russian leadership into nuclear war. The concerns of the law are with choices, reasons, intentions. Only an intentional act is a crime; a murder is a murder not because the victim is dead but because this death was intentionally brought about. We give our own reasons to explain our own behavior, and we use the reasons of others to predict or influence what they do. To ensure that four people will assemble on a tennis court to play a doubles match, we concern ourselves with their knowledge and their desires. We make sure that they wish to play and that they know the time and place. In education, we fill children's minds with the knowledge that they will need to guide rational thought, from the steps of a geometric proof to a balanced appreciation of the rights of others. In politics, we act to change the reasons of others—we debate, negotiate, persuade, argue, bargain, or bribe.

This rational perspective is certainly natural, and in our daily lives it is very effective. One person is out shopping for clothes; another is at work; one is preparing dinner; a fourth is landing from a trip to South America. Yet with one small sentence typed into an email program, it can be ensured that all four individuals will converge at the same place at the same time, carrying racquets and ready for tennis. We are so used to it that we forget to think how remarkable it is that four animals can coordinate their activity in this way.

When we explain by reason, it is perhaps apt to say that we think of ourselves as subjects rather than objects. From this perspective, we are free agents, the causes and not the effects in the world we inhabit. We evaluate options, choose as we wish, and are responsible and accountable for those choices. If we are asked why we did something, the explanations we give will refer to the reasons we had. Free agents do as they wish; they do as their reasons dictate.

Hidden behind this, though, is a different perspective. Sometimes, we explain ourselves in a different way. We acknowledge that we forgot to stop on the way home to pick up milk. We say that we drove foolishly because we were angry with the children. Many years ago, I conducted research on absent-minded slips and how they happen. My favorite was, "I filled the washing machine with porridge." (Even more pleasing was the woman who, responding to this item on a questionnaire, said that she did this sort of thing, not "never," not "rarely," not "often," but "nearly all the time." Her clothes, however, appeared normal.) In these cases, suddenly we do not explain behavior as a free choice, as the intention to achieve something by a certain means. Instead, we are saying something about the choice process itself. We are acknowledging that reasoning has its limits—that sometimes it goes well, but sometimes it does not.

For the science of mind and brain, this second perspective is central. From this perspective, we are biological machines with biological limits. Indeed, we think and reason, we form wishes, beliefs, plans, and intentions. But these reasons are not created in the abstract—they are created by the machine. In explaining human behavior, understanding reasons is only half the story. The other half is understanding the machine by which reasons are made. This is the half that this book is about.

From this perspective, what we want to know is how the machine works. What are reason and thought, and how do they work in the human mind and brain? What is human intelligence: How does it extend the intelligence of other animals? How does it relate to the intelligence of thinking computers? How can it arise from billions of tiny nerve cells communicating by brief electrical impulses?

In some ways science comes naturally. We find it natural to apply a perspective of objective inquiry to the understanding of molecules, planets, forces, diseases—indeed, almost anything at all. In my view, this comes easily because science is simply a more systematic version of our natural, everyday fascination with knowledge—with a fundamental understanding of how our world works. It is sometimes suggested that babies are born as natural scientists. Crawling across a lawn, the baby touches a thistle. He pulls back . . . reaches out carefully to test again . . . pulls back again . . . tests again. He is born to observe and to fill his mind with useful knowledge, with the knowledge he will use to navigate through life. As Francis Bacon put it, "Ipsa scientia potestas est"—in itself, knowledge is power. In science, our natural fascination with knowledge is simply put into organized, institutionalized form.

Natural though we find it in most cases, the objective analysis of science comes much less naturally when we apply it to our own minds. There is an unsettling tension between our usual perspective on ourselves—as rational agents looking from the inside out—and the opposite perspective of science, observing the machine from the outside in.

As soon as we look at ourselves from outside in, clear cracks appear in the "free agent" impression. Of course, it is quite obvious that our behavior is not at all free and unconstrained. Instead, like any other entity, we have our own properties, potentialities, and limits. Our behavior is explained, not only by the reasons we had, but by the limited reasoning machinery we have at our disposal.

Perspectives become more compelling with use, and after more than thirty years as an experimental psychologist, looking at myself and those around me as object rather than subject, it is now quite hard for me to recapture the sense of how I used to think. Quite often, though, the opposing perspectives clash. For example, a few years ago I was attending a conference in New York. In a bar I was introduced to a neuroscientist who worked in a distantly related field, and soon we were in a debate. Putting some key fact onto the table, she said, "I'm absolutely certain that this is true." "Aha," I replied, "but what's the correlation between your confidence and your accuracy?" The question is reasonable but impolite, and slightly too late I realized that I had stepped over the brink between psychologist and normal person. In everyday life we do not like it when our own reason machines are analyzed and questioned; the outside in perspective is unsettling (at best). But for the science of the reason machine, just such questions are the daily fare.

I have always been fond of this anti-psychology joke. Two psychologists pass in the street. One says, "Hello!" The other one continues on his way, thinking, "I wonder why he said that?"

Let me begin with a small example of the limits of the free agent, an example of irresistibly doing something against our will. In psychology it is called the Stroop effect, after the American psychologist John Ridley Stroop, who first described it in 1935.[1] A person is asked to scan as quickly as possible down a sheet of paper, calling out the colors of everything he sees. (To avoid repetitions of "he or she," I shall make my imaginary person a man in all these examples. Also, in line with the fact that this man is now the subject matter of investigation, I shall follow the convention of experimental psychology and call him "the subject." To be consistent with what I just said, I might have called him "the object"—but even experimental psychology has not generally gone that far. Usually, to make the results more reliable, psychological experiments gather data over many repetitions of the same task; we call these repetitions "trials.") The subject knows he will be timed. His task is to finish each trial as quickly as possible. The experimenter sits with a stopwatch to see how fast it can be done.

In the first version, the items on the page are rows of Xs written in different-colored inks. The subject goes down the list from top to bottom, calling out the colors as fast as possible; when he gets to the bottom, the result is written down. In the second version, there is one small change. Now the items on the page are not just rows of colored Xs; they are colored words that spell out color names. Specifically, the words spelled are different from the colors of the inks—so that, for example, the subject might see BLUE written in orange or GREEN written in purple. For the subject this should not matter. He is not asked to read the words; in fact, he should ignore them. As before, he just has to go down the list naming all the ink colors as fast as possible. Suddenly, though, this is much harder to do. Every time he tries to name an ink color, the word he is looking at also pops into mind. He slows down, makes false starts, may even read an occasional word out loud. Free will? This experiment shows that we cannot even choose to avoid the simple act of reading.

Experimental psychology commonly focuses on such limits or constraints on mental ability. In part, this is because limits are often helpful in understanding how something works. In part, it is because limits are constantly brought to our attention in practical situations, and bypassing them can be an important practical concern. Though we are rarely asked to name colors as quickly as possible, especially not when these colors belong to conflicting words, we are often re-quired to do several things at once. In the early 1950s, psychologists became interested in our limited ability to divide our attention. This interest had its origins during World War II, when psychologists had been employed to address practical military problems of this sort: air-traffic controllers dealing with simultaneous radio calls or fighter pilots handling multiple cockpit controls. How much information could a person actually process at one time? How did this depend on the way that the information was presented or what sort of information it was? Again, the results of these experiments show severe limits on our ability to do what we want.

Through the 1950s, our limited ability to process simultaneous events was investigated by such psychologists as Colin Cherry, Christopher Poulton, and Donald Broadbent.[2] In a typical experiment, the subject heard two simultaneous speech messages, one arriving through a headphone on the left ear, the other through a headphone on the right. To demand careful attention to one message, perhaps the one on the right, the subject was asked to repeat the message back continuously as it came in. After a minute or two of this, he was stopped and asked questions about the other message. With his attention focused on one message, how much did he manage to pick up from the other?

By and large, the answer from these experiments was: astonishingly little. Usually, the subject would not know if the ignored message had concerned air transport or classical literature. In fact, he would not even know that, halfway through, the message had changed from English to German or to speech played backwards. To allow the subject to pick up anything at all from the second message, the most extreme changes had to be made. For example, usually he would notice if, for significant lengths of time, the spoken message was changed to a continuous tone. Similar results were found if, while repeating back one message, the subject was also asked to detect occasional target words—perhaps color words—in either message. For the message he was repeating, the targets would usually be detected, but for the other message, most targets were missed.[3]

In 1960 an intriguing variation on this experiment was designed by a young University of Oxford student named Anne Treisman. As usual, the subject was set to repeat back one message—perhaps the one on the right. As usual, he knew little of the other, in this case the one on the left. At an unpredictable moment, the two messages switched sides. The message that had previously been arriving on the right now switched to the left, whereas the message that had previously been ignored on the left now switched to the right. This was all irrelevant to the subject, whose instruction was to keep on repeating whatever message came from the right, no matter what it was. Nevertheless, in a good proportion of trials, the subject stumbled as the switch occurred and even for a word or two continued to follow the previous message, though now it was arriving on the left. The experiment raises intriguing questions. If a person cannot even tell whether the left ear has normal English or reversed German speech, how can he (at some level) "know" when the left ear continues the sense of the message he has just been following—knowledge sufficient to cause him to break the rule he has been given and switch to repeating things from the wrong ear? Again, such experiments point up severe limits on our mental activity—limits on our ability to do or to achieve things we firmly wished and intended to achieve.[4]

Faced with examples like these, our natural human reaction is to shift somewhat the goalposts of free will. Obviously, we reason, our minds/brains have some basic, low-level limitations. Of course, we have always known that we cannot do fifteen things at once. Really, though, this is not what we mean by free will and rationality. At a higher level, we remain rational agents who freely choose the course of action that is best.

So let's move up to some of the limits on reason itself. Again, experimental psychology can provide textbooks full of examples, but I will just give one that I especially like. It comes from one of the great wise men of British psychology, Peter Wason, and a series of experiments carried out in the early 1960s.[5]

In these experiments, the subject simply has to discover the rule that is used to generate sets of three numbers. He is given the first set of three: "2, 4, 6." He is told that he must discover the rule by generating additional sets of three numbers. Each time he generates a set, the experimenter will tell him whether it obeys the rule. Then, when the subject is *sure* that he knows the rule, and not before, he should stop the experiment and announce what the rule is. He can take as much time as he likes.

The experiment typically unfolds this way. The subject generates a set like "4, 6, 8." He is told that it satisfies the rule. He tries "10, 12, 14" and is told again that it obeys the rule. If particularly cautious, the subject may try "1, 3, 5" and even "1022, 1024, 1026," both of which are equally successful. At this point he announces that he is terminating the experiment and that the rule is "three numbers increasing in 2s."

He is told that this is not the rule and is asked to continue.

At this point things begin to drift out of hand. The experiment can continue for half an hour or more, as the subject traps himself in a spiral of increasingly elaborate hypotheses. A common next step is to imagine that the middle number must be the average of the first and last. The subject tries "3, 6, 9" and "13, 27, 41." Or the subject may begin to think that the first number doesn't matter; only the second increase by 2 is important. He generates "1, 4, 6" and "27, 32, 34." When he hears again that his choices match the experimenter's rule, it seems impossible that the baroque rule he has thought of could be wrong, so again he stops the experiment and announces it. Again he is told that he is wrong, but surely such a specific rule that generated correct examples must have been near the truth? The subject now constructs an even more complex rule, attempting to accommodate

the structure of the previous rule while adding some new, apparently arbitrary twist. Arbitrary though it is, the new examples it generates usually obeys the rule, and the web gains a new thread.

In fact, the rule of the experiment is simply "three numbers in increasing order." How on earth can a rule that is so simple be so difficult to discover, even by subjects recruited from a university science department? As Wason explained, the answer is a bias to confirmation rather than disconfirmation. Under the influence of this bias, we are blind to most possible explanations for the data at hand. How rational are we when we ignore what is glaringly obvious?

Confirmation bias works like this. When we start with "2, 4, 6," the "increase in 2s" rule is our obvious first thought. (It is an interesting further topic why this particular rule is the "obvious" one.) With this hypothesis in mind, confirmation bias leads to generation of further candidates that *satisfy* the hypothesis. When these candidates are also correct, it is impossible to believe that the hypothesis is wrong— the more so, the more complex it becomes. The problem is that we have given essentially no thought to all the other, equally sensible hypotheses that were not our first, preferred candidate (including the correct one). With the idea of other hypotheses in mind, perhaps we should have tried the strategy that actually works for problems like this—the strategy, in fact, that is widely lauded as the method of choice for science in general. This is the attempt to *disconfirm*, by generating examples that *do not* satisfy the original hypothesis. This strategy might have led to such triplets as "1, 2, 3" and then "2, 4, 17"—found to satisfy the experimenter's rule, disconfirming the original "increase in 2s" hypothesis, and leading directly away from the spiral of apparent confirmation for increasingly complex, increasingly irrelevant ideas.

Once seriously examined, the idea of ourselves as optimal reasoning agents seems absurd. Its appeal, nevertheless, is profound.

Another of the fathers of modern psychology, Herbert Simon, won the Nobel Prize in economics for pointing out this absurdity. In the economics of the first half of the twentieth century, a fictitious Economic Man assessed available options and made optimal choices to maximize wealth. In the 1950s—the dawn of modern computing and modern consideration of how information is used as the basis for decision—Simon pointed out that real economic decisions do not work this way. In real-life problems, generally speaking, the information is not available to determine which option is optimal, and even if it were, we would lack the computational or mental resources to evaluate it. Instead of choosing the *best* option, what we do in real decision-making is choose an option that is *good enough*. In Simon's terms, we do not *optimize* but *satisfice*; a concept of global rationality is replaced by *bounded rationality*—rational choices within the constraints of the information available and our power to use it. Though he could have used almost anything, Simon used chess to illustrate his point. In some computer programs, chess can indeed be played by evaluating every alternative move down to some depth of possible outcomes, then choosing the one with the best prospect. Evidently, when humans play, we do nothing like this. Instead we satisfice—we consider options until we find one that is *good enough*—with an acceptable level of gain or probability of victory—and go with that. As reflected in Simon's Nobel Prize, an economics based on real, human rationality differs profoundly from an economics based on abstract, global, ideal evaluation of options. Later (chapter 5), we shall return in detail to Simon and the use of computer programs to simulate human problem-solving and thought.[6]

I shall finish this section with one more example, both because it is striking in itself and because it directly touches on the mismatch between our actual selves and our beliefs about ourselves. The example may be familiar—it appears in every introductory textbook and popular presentation of psychology. However, I have something to add that I particularly like but is less often mentioned. The experiment, conducted by Stanley Milgram in the 1960s, concerns social pressure.[7]

In the Milgram experiment, there were one experimenter, one subject, and one stooge who also appeared to be a subject. The real subject was told that he and the other "subject" would participate in an experiment on learning. Specifically, the other subject (actually the stooge) would have to learn something, and whenever he failed, the real subject would have to punish him. He would do this by administering electric shocks from a machine. If learning continued to fail, he would have to make the shocks stronger.

The experiment began, and the stooge began to fail. As instructed, the real subject began to administer electric shocks. (So he thought. Of course, there never were any real shocks.) At first, these appeared to be mild, but as the experiment continued and the subject turned up the strength, the stooge began to feign serious distress. Naturally enough, the real subject at some stage would begin to suggest that the experiment should be discontinued. This suggestion was always answered by the instruction that the experiment must continue, and the shock must be turned up.

What Milgram found was that people went remarkably far into this experiment. Even when the stooge was begging for things to stop, even when the subject's dial had been turned into a zone marked "danger," and even though the subject himself was seriously horrified, still he was told that "the experiment must continue," and still he went on turning up the strength and administering the shocks. The experiment bears fascinatingly on social control and on handing responsibility to others, and it shows how normal, decent people can do appalling things in the face of an accepted social structure and an acknowledged path of authority.

This is interesting, but it is not the end. In follow-ups to Milgram's work, other experimenters have addressed the mismatch between reality and belief.[8] This time, the subjects are not put into the experiment and tricked. They are told all about Milgram's experiment, about how it worked, and about the typical levels of shock that normal subjects could be led to administer. But then they are asked, "If you had been in that experiment, would you have given the shock?" And now—even knowing all that they do, about the experiment and about how people behave in it—still almost everybody answers, "No." They understand that most people can be led to do something quite incredible . . . but still they believe that they themselves would never have done it. What a lovely demonstration of the tension between our two perspectives, inside out and outside in. Looking from the outside in, we know full well how limited, biased, and constrained the human mind is. Looking from the inside out, we still know that we ourselves are responsible and free.

The denial of free will is often felt as somehow belittling. The basic sense is that, if our choices are constrained by our biological hardware—by the genes that directed our development and the experiences that made us who we are—then somehow they are no longer our own, free choices at all. Though many people feel this way, to my mind it is a case of being fooled by language. To me, the sense in which psychology denies freedom is not at all the sense in which people feel that they have it.

The key thing is to recognize something hidden in the word "free." This is the implication of some specific constraint that the person or action is free of. I know what it means for a person to be free of jail or an unwanted boyfriend or a concern for the future. I do not know what it would mean to be free in the abstract . . . free of what? So, when we say that we have free will, what are we saying that we are free of? I think we are claiming freedom to make our own minds up, to make our own choices. Certainly this means a firm commitment to the belief that, ultimately, nobody else can force us to think or even act in a way we choose not to. But do we also mean that we are free of *ourselves?* Surely not. Who has "our own mind" if not ourselves?

Now, all that experimental psychology offers is a different perspective on ourselves. Viewed from the inside out, we are independent people, freely choosing our actions. Viewed from the outside in, a "person" is a biological entity subject to its own rules of operation, mysterious though these rules may be. The views may seem incompatible, but in fact, they are only different views of the same person. When people claim freedom, they are not really claiming freedom from themselves. It is the same thing to say that they are not claiming freedom from all the complex of factors and constraints that make them who they are.

Free will is generally taken to conflict with determinism—with the idea that our choices arise from the factors that made us. In my view there is no conflict, as long as we are careful with what we mean. By "free will" I do not think we mean that our choices are free of ourselves. They can be free of any or all other constraints, but not of ourselves. Accordingly, it is simply irrelevant to ask how we ourselves come to be. We have already accepted that, whatever the answer to that question, it has no bearing on a sense of "freedom" from all that is *not* ourselves.

I would say much the same about responsibility. When we "hold a person responsible," this means that we will judge them by what they choose to do and call them to account for those decisions. From the outside-in perspective, it is true that the person we are judging is the way he or she is for many reasons of biology and personal history— but this is just a different view of the same entity we are judging. It in no way changes the judgment that this entity is good or bad, desirable or undesirable, to be applauded or punished. A few years ago, a friend and I thought we should make a fortune by writing a book to explain how people's brains made them do all the things they knew they shouldn't. This book was going to be full of sex, indiscretion, and chocolate. We thought we would call it, "It's Not Your Fault—It's Your Brain." Unfortunately for the plan, I could never really have lived with that title. Possibly less appealingly, I would have been forced to go for: "Yes, It's Your Brain—But It's Still Your Fault."

Now it is time to start on the main story. This is the story of a search for the origins of intelligence—the intelligence that, in the Havana plaza, allows the police to watch for traffic infringements, the mother to usher her children to their destination, the driver to emerge from the street entrance.

The story has many parts. A large part will be neurobiology: brain structure and function, how brains support behavior, how thought and reason change when the brain is damaged. A part will be computer science: the enterprise of artificial intelligence and the light it casts on how reason is constructed. The story begins, though, with pure experimental psychology—with a stable regularity of the human mind, learned, not from the study of brain or computer, but from the systematic observation and measurement of human behavior itself.

Chapter 2 **A Regularity**

The understanding of intelligence has many sides. The first part of my story is the troubled idea of *differences* in ability from one person to the next. Often, this is taken to be the central question of intelligence, which I think it is not. Still, study of this question has led to some remarkably stable and informative discoveries. The study of differences, it turns out, is a valuable entry point to a much bigger picture.

Differences in ability raise immediate concerns. A friend once told me that my interest in this question would make "everybody in America hate me." I should like to hope not; later I shall suggest that the social concerns that make the question inflammatory are really quite separate from the scientific concerns that make it informative. Here my concern is with the science and with the clues it gives us to the structure and workings of the human mind.

In this chapter, I will be talking a good deal about Charles Spearman, the theoretical father of this field and, in the early part of the twentieth century, one of the founding fathers of experimental psychology itself. Though some of Spearman's basic ideas remain highly familiar today, his original work, I imagine, is barely read. This is a shame, because the original experiments and theoretical analysis are spectacular, fascinating, and powerful.

Much of the worst confusion in experimental psychology comes from terminology. "Intelligence" is a striking case in point—perhaps, indeed, the most striking case. A hundred years after Spearman, the field is still filled with debates about what intelligence is and what it is not. Is intelligence strictly cognitive, or is it also emotional? Is memory an aspect of intelligence, or is it something separate? What is the real essence of what it means to be "intelligent"?

As Spearman himself pointed out with great precision, questions like these have no real meaning. They are strictly questions of terminology, not content—questions not about how the world is but about what we will call things. "Intelligence" is simply a word from everyday language. Coming as it does from a rough everyday vocabulary for talking about ourselves, we have every reason to suspect that it will have no "real essence" at all. There is no very exact meaning, no very exact way to specify what does and does not count. Accordingly, we are free to call emotion or memory a part of "intelligence," or not to. It really makes no difference to an actual understanding of these different aspects of our minds.

Truthfully, we tend to say that almost anything that is successful, useful, or effective is "intelligent." Sometimes when we call something "stupid" we mean little beyond dislike ("I'm sick of this stupid rain"). Car manufacturers tell us that their product is intelligence on wheels. We call a little girl intelligent when she recites the nursery rhyme she has learned, and a dog intelligent when it cocks up its ear and runs to the front door as car wheels crunch on the gravel. Certainly it might be said that everything a brain does is a form of intelligence, from the intelligence of an insect to the intelligence of a party host or mathematician.

In my opinion, it is going backwards for science to try and "capture the essence" of everyday concepts. We may expect everyday concepts to be loose, ill-defined, flexible. We expect systematic observation to come up with harder things that we can actually work with. When psychology attempts to find the essence of such concepts as attention, memory, or intelligence, I am reminded of the prescientific elements of earth, water, fire, and air. It is as if a chemist, having established the periodic table, then peers at it to ask: "Now—where's the earth, water, fire, and air?"

When we think about Spearman's ideas, we must remember that they are science. We should not ask them to represent "the essence of intelligence." We should not ask that they capture the full richness of human achievement and human thought (what psychological theory could do that?). We cannot usefully ask what "intelligence" really means—but we can usefully ask what discovery Spearman made, what theory he proposed to explain it, and how that theory stands up against subsequent observations.

We must begin with a basic statistical idea—the idea of correlation. The correlation problem is illustrated in figure 1. Imagine we have forty things—perhaps forty people (though they could be anything). For each person, we measure two properties or characteristics. For example, we might measure height and weight, but because these properties could be anything, we can call them X and Y. Now in the graph we plot one property against the other. Each person in the graph corresponds to a single dot. The position of the dot shows both the value of X and the value of Y for that person.

Figure 1a shows the first example. Here the dots form a circular cloud, meaning that X and Y are completely unrelated. In statistics we say that they are uncorrelated; measuring X tells you nothing about what Y is likely to be. (You may think that, even if X and Y are completely unrelated, the cloud will not be circular if the scales for

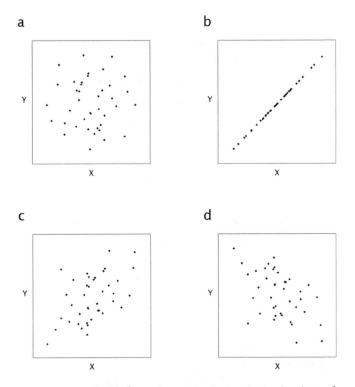

Figure 1. Four types of correlation. Within each panel, values of X vary from low (left) to high (right), and values of Y vary from low (bottom) to high (top). The four panels show four very different relationships between X and Y.

X and Y are very different. For example, if X is measured on a scale from 0 to 100 but Y is measured only on a scale from 0 to 10, then we will end up with a long, horizontal ellipse. For convenience, however, a statistician always makes the scales the same for X and Y before working on correlations. We don't need to worry about the exact method for doing this.) In figure 1b, the situation is reversed— the dots all fall along a perfectly straight line. This means that they are perfectly correlated—if you measure X for a new person, the graph tells you exactly what Y should be. Figure 1c describes something intermediate—a very common result with real measurements. Here the dots form neither a circular cloud nor a perfect straight line but something in between. This would be the case, for example, for height and weight. On average, tall people weigh more than short people, but even for a fixed height, some people weigh more than others. Put another way, measuring a person's height allows you to make some prediction about how heavy he or she is likely to be, but not a perfect prediction. Finally, there is the possibility of such cases as figure 1d. Here, there is a relationship between X and Y, but it is reversed—a higher value on X tends to go with a lower value on Y. For example, people with more money are less likely to drive old cars. If X is a person's income, and Y is the age of their car, then the graph will look like figure 1d.

In statistics, the strength of correlation is measured by a single number, ranging from +1 through 0 to −1. Values of +1 and −1 correspond to the two opposite cases of perfect prediction, +1 with all points on a line sloping upward (high values of X mean high values of Y—fig. 1b), −1 the same but with the line sloping downward (high values of X mean low values of Y). A value of 0 means no correlation at all: a perfectly circular cloud (fig. 1a). Values between 0 and +1 or between 0 and −1 mean some degree of correlation, either positive or negative. In figure 1c, for example, the correlation is +0.5, whereas in figure 1d, it is −0.5. Again, we do not need to worry about the exact method for calculating this number. All we need to know is that, the farther the value is from 0, the stronger is the correlation—the better one number can be predicted from the other.

Spearman's original paper on human abilities appeared in the *American Journal of Psychology* in 1904.[1] In that volume, Spearman's paper is sandwiched between a discussion of the soul and an account of "the psychology of the English sparrow." In 1904, methods for measuring correlation, which now we take for granted, were under active development. Spearman himself had just published a major contribution. In particular, he had analyzed how correlation must depend on the stability of measurement for X and Y themselves. (Imagine that you measure weight with bad scales that give very different values for the same person measured twice in succession. The correlation with height must be reduced, because the measurement of weight is now less predictable in general. Spearman made a mathematical analysis of this problem and showed how "true" correlations could be mathematically corrected for unreliability of measurement.) Now he applied his methods to a central question about the human mind. How well does a person's ability to do one thing—for example, to learn Latin—predict his or her ability to do another—for example, to hit a cricket ball?

In fact, Spearman did not use cricket, though he did use Latin. In this first experiment—the forerunner of an enormous research effort, first in his own laboratory and continuing around the world to the present day—Spearman actually compared school achievement with the ability to make elementary sensory discriminations. In two schools, he obtained various measures of academic ability—ratings from teachers, exam grades in a range of subjects, and so on. Then each child received separate tests of sensory ability—for example, the ability to discriminate two tones, two weights, or two shades of gray. Spearman used the new methods of correlation to ask about relations between all these different measures—between every pair of exam results, between each exam and each sensory discrimination, and so on for every pair of measurements in the experiment.

What might we expect to find in an experiment like this? On the one hand, it is probably a general belief that some people are "brighter," "sharper," "more intelligent" than others. Surely we should at least expect a tendency for the same children to excel at different school subjects. On the other hand, we also live in a world where people evidently have their own special abilities and aptitudes. We do not expect the linguist and the cricketer to be the same. Reasoning this way, we might expect rather low correlations—at least for the comparison between academic achievement and sensory ability.

Spearman's first great result was that all the correlations tended to be positive. Some were higher than others. Certainly we know now that the everyday intuition is correct and that correlations between different school subjects will usually be higher than correlations between academic achievement and sensory discrimination. Still, the result was that every data plot looked like figure 1c. To some extent at least, people doing well on one thing were also more likely to do well on others. For the first time, Spearman's results placed this result on an objective footing—and gave a measure of exactly how true it was.

For the next step, Spearman made an extraordinary leap of imagination and method. Achievements in different school subjects, he reasoned, might be regarded as different attempts to measure some general tendency toward academic strength. Similarly, accuracy of discrimination in different sensory modalities might be regarded as different attempts to measure a general discrimination ability. Thinking of the problem in this way, Spearman could bring into play his new methods for correcting correlations for unreliability of measurement. Each individual score would be regarded as an unreliable attempt to get at the true, underlying general academic ability or general sensory ability. Spearman could thus correct the measured correlations and derive an estimated correlation between the underlying general abilities. Over the subsequent hundred years, statistical methods for doing this sort of thing have become much more sophisticated. "Factor analysis," for example, now used throughout science and engineering to analyze patterns of correlational data, is a direct descendant of Spearman's work. Simple though his methods were, however, Spearman's analysis delivered a remarkable result. When estimated by his methods, academic ability and sensory ability showed a correlation of approximately 1. In other words—using some mathematics to look beneath the surface correlations of individual tests and to estimate a *general* ability in two quite different domains (school and sensory experiments)—it seemed that these two abilities were one and the same. The people who did well across the board at school were the same as the people who did well across the board in sensory discriminations.

The theory that Spearman proposed to explain these findings was another imaginative leap. Suppose we measure not just academic ability or sensory discrimination but *any* mental ability or achievement—speed of decision, ability to remember, ability to solve technical problems, musical or artistic ability—anything at all. For each one of these abilities, Spearman proposed that there will be two sorts of contribution. One is some contribution from a *general factor* in each person's makeup—something the person uses in *anything* he or she undertakes. Initially, Spearman called this "general intelligence," and though this term has stuck, he himself later abandoned it for the sorts of reasons I gave at the beginning of the chapter. Instead, he preferred to call it simply the general factor, or g. Second, there will be contributions from one or more *specific factors*—individual skills, talents, or other factors that are specific to the particular ability measured, such as memory or art, with little or no influence on other activities. People will vary randomly on their level of g (how effectively the general factor operates). They will also vary randomly on all possible specific factors; Spearman called these the s factors.

For any ability we measure, the two factors combine to determine each person's overall success. If we measure, for example, success in remembering chess positions, this will partly reflect g (a general ability to do all tests well) and partly s (a specific ability with chess positions, certainly determined at least in part by knowledge of chess). A person can obtain the same score because he or she is high on g though low on s, high on s though low on g, or intermediate on both. The theory thus captures both of the everyday intuitions I outlined above. Indeed it is true that, to some extent at least, the same people tend to do well at whatever they undertake. In an experiment like Spearman's, all correlations are positive. On the theory, this reflects the global influence of g. Just as Spearman's analysis suggested, this general ability to do well is the same no matter what tests are used to measure it. Equally, though, people also have their individual abilities to do well in specific areas. Although different kinds of tests have some positive correlation, these correlations are generally far from 1. This means many people who, for example, do quite well in Greek but quite poorly in discrimination of weights. The multitude of specific abilities is captured in the s factors.

Though the name of Spearman is universally associated with g, he himself was never in doubt of the equal significance of s. Even in his first paper, he was clear that the relative importance of g and s varies widely from one ability to another. Some—for example, ability in Greek in one of the first schools Spearman used—are mainly g and very little s. Some—for example, music—are the reverse, with very little g at all. One of the great merits Spearman saw in his work was the opportunity to be explicit and quantitative in such assessments. Here from the 1904 paper is a characteristically Edwardian comment on the potential for practical application (in fact, Spearman did later work for the armed forces):

> Instead of continuing ineffectively to protest that high marks in
> Greek syntax are no test as to the capacity of men to command

troops or to administer provinces, we shall at last accurately determine the precise accuracy of the various means of testing General
Intelligence, and then we shall in an equally positive objective
manner ascertain the exact relative importance of this General Intelligence as compared with the other characteristics desirable for the
particular post which the candidate is to assume (such as any required Specific Intelligences, also Instruction, Force of Will, Physical
Constitution, Honesty, Zeal, etc.).[2]

For every performance that a person can produce, then, there is a
mixture of g and s—with g reflecting some "general factor" brought
into play in everything the person does, and the s factors reflecting
an uncountable horde of specific skills, abilities, and other personal
characteristics.

After his first paper, Spearman ran many other experiments cor-
relating performances in different kinds of activity. Similar experiments have been run thousands of times, using every possible variety
of task or test. Psychologists have looked at vocabulary, mental folding
of paper shapes, every conceivable variety of memory, arithmetical
and logical skills, reaction time, ability to see things in a brief flash,
filling in outlines of lampshades with as many designs as possible,
route finding and maze tracing, moving the hand as fast as possible
between one place and another, using codes, and much more. The
limit of this enterprise is set simply by the limit of psychologists'
imagination and perseverance.

As Spearman anticipated, the result is always the same. No matter
how many tasks are designed, and how carefully they are separated in
terms of content, mental operation, or method of performance measurement, the result is always repeated. As long as the number of people
tested is large (correlations become more stable the more observations
are made), and as long as these people represent a sensible, broad sam-

ple of the normal population, all the dozens or hundreds of correlations that are measured will be positive. Some will be weak (I already
said that music, for example, is almost all s, meaning that it correlates
only very weakly with everything else). Some will be much stronger—
this will be important shortly. But even in the hands of psychologists
who strongly wished to find something different, the basic result remains. Technically the result is called "positive manifold"—a large set
of correlations among different tests that are all positive, reflecting a
global tendency for the same people to do well at different things.

In my opinion, this is really rather a surprising result. Perhaps we
knew all along that the same child who does well in physics is also
likely to be goodish or good in French. But did we really know that
the same also applies to remembering a phone number or pressing
a key as fast as possible when a light comes on? Certainly, we could
not have hoped to guess at the *exact extent* to which all these different relations hold. People sometimes wonder whether experimental
psychology is really science. Here, simple measurements of behavior
tell us something new, remarkable, and well-defined—something
demanding to be explained.

It follows from the mathematics of Spearman's approach that a battery of tests—for example, a test of memory for lists of words, a test
of reaction time, a test of vocabulary, a test of spatial navigation, and a
test of dividing attention—can be used to derive a value of g for every
person tested. In other words, we can measure each person's g level.
Though there are several mathematical methods for doing this, the essential intuition behind them is very simple. Indeed, we have already
seen the idea in Spearman's first analysis of school achievement and
sensory discrimination. If a person is high on g, this person will tend
to do well overall. Any single test will reflect this only poorly, since it
may also be strongly influenced by its s. However, the more tests one

gives—and in particular, the more very different tests—the more it should happen that the *overall* or average performance is mainly determined by *g*. In fact, the simplest approach to measuring *g* would just be to average together measures of achievement on all the tests in the battery—and the larger the battery, the better that will work.

This idea that all kinds of tests have a common influence—the person's level of *g*—leads to another striking prediction, again anticipated in Spearman's first experiment. Suppose that one constructs two entirely unrelated test batteries. The first might be the battery I just described, with tests of memory, reaction time, vocabulary, navigation, and attention. For the second battery, we might put in discrimination of weights, solving jigsaw puzzles, recognizing objects photographed from unusual views, generating uses for a brick, arithmetic. On the face of it these two batteries are measuring completely different things, so there would be no strong reason to suppose that a person who does well on one battery will also do well on the other. According to Spearman's theory, however, it does not matter what tests are put into a battery. The more tests are included, the more exactly all batteries will converge to measure the same *g*. Spearman called this theoretical possibility of measuring *g* equally accurately by many different methods "indifference of the indicator." Bold though the prediction was, it is now known to be largely borne out. As long as two batteries of tests are reasonably large and diverse, average performance on one is strongly correlated with average performance on the other. The *g* derived from one battery is thus very much the same as the *g* derived from the second—just as Spearman found comparing school ability with sensory discrimination.

At the same time that Spearman was working, there had also grown up a strong tradition for practical measurement of "intelligence," especially in schools. Following on from early work by a French psychologist, Alfred Binet, a growing number of "intelligence tests" were developed, using the basic method of measuring how well each child did many different things. It is this work that led to the idea of "intelligence quotient," or IQ, and to the typical IQ tests that we see today. Remarkably, these tests were developed with no real theoretical justification. Indeed, psychologists through the first part of the twentieth century were severely taxed by the question of what abilities were really parts of "intelligence" and therefore what tasks should be included in a valid "intelligence test." Should memory be included? and reasoning? and speed? If so, in what proportions? Should one estimate "intelligence" with two parts of reasoning to one part of memory to half a part of speed or some other unknown combination? (Spearman has a lovely description of this conceptual chaos in his 1927 book, *The Abilities of Man*.)[3] The theory of g solves the problem in a surprising way. It says that the question does not matter. *Any* diverse set of tasks will serve to measure g. Thus IQ tests have retained their practical utility over the years, despite their impression of jumbling together a semi-random mixture of apparently different things.

At the beginning of this chapter I suggested that our everyday concept of "intelligence" has little definite meaning. It is flexible, sometimes metaphorical. It is hard to suppose that it refers to any one thing in particular.

In contrast to this, Spearman's concept of g is something definite. It is a theoretical construct proposed to explain particular facts (the existence of positive manifold). The theory specifies precise ways to measure g, and when those procedures are followed, the result is a stable measurement with known properties. Is it "intelligence"? This, I would say, is simply the wrong question. In some ways, g is more than intelligence—more definite, more objective, better defined. In some ways, it is less, since a concept such as g can hardly capture all the many different things that may sometimes be called "intelligent."

As we would hope from science, we have produced a new idea. It is not unrelated to what we had before—but neither is it the same.

Certainly, the results of these experiments are interesting. The idea of g hints at something fundamentally important about the human mind and brain. But how important is it in people's actual lives? Are we only talking about ability to solve meaningless laboratory puzzles? Or even about something that may matter in education but not in most other aspects of our lives?

We may look at this question in different ways. I will just mention two. Over the past hundred years, literally thousands of experiments have investigated methods for predicting how well people will perform at work. In total, millions of people have been tested in every conceivable job from the simplest and most unskilled to the most complex. The basic aim is to devise tests or methods giving the best possible chance of hiring effective employees. Every conceivable type of method has been examined—interviews, references, on-the-job performance tests, personality measures, basic ability tests, graphology (trying to read a person's nature from their handwriting). The sheer volume and breadth of resulting data have required development of new branches of statistics to combine and assess the results. There are few things in the modern world that have been more thoroughly investigated, and the results tell a clear and quite astonishing story.[4]

Some methods work reasonably well. The best is to make a direct measurement of ability on the job. To select a good bricklayer, for example, the best thing to assess is how well this person lays bricks. That assessment will correlate above 0.5 with later productivity. Some methods are useless: graphology, for instance—although in such countries as Israel, graphology has been a popular basis for hiring decisions.

Just behind actually measuring performance on the job comes a test of general cognitive ability—essentially, a test of g. For completely unskilled jobs, this may correlate only about 0.2 or 0.3 with later productivity. For a job of average complexity, the correlation is around 0.5, and for the most complex jobs, it approaches 0.6. Psychologists have become used to the power of g and may not find this surprising. On reflection, though—how can this possibly be? To select a bricklayer, we can ask if he or she can lay bricks, or we can spend an hour giving an apparently arbitrary ragbag of artificial tests and then just average the results? And these two methods work about equally well?? Surely these facts tell us something quite remarkable about the human mind.

Here is another telling observation. Suppose we assemble a long list of possible jobs and ask people to rate how desirable those jobs are. We produce a ranking of jobs in terms of how much the average person would like to have them, from top to bottom. Now we produce a second ranking—in order of the average IQ of people who actually hold those jobs. What we find is that the two orders agree almost perfectly. In fact, the correlation between the two is above 0.9.[5] The more that people want a particular job, the more that job is actually populated by people with high g scores. Whatever this is, it is certainly something with a profound effect on people's lives.

There is another thing that can be done with the mathematics of Spearman's theory. Imagine again that we have administered a battery of tasks—perhaps ten of them—to a large group of people. The result is a list of correlations between each task and all the others. If we used ten tasks, there will actually be forty-five of these correlations. As we have seen, in real data they will all turn out to be positive, though some will be much higher than others. As a rough rule of thumb, the highest we will see in practice will be around 0.6, while the lowest may be around 0.1. (This is presuming that we have tried to make the tasks as different as we can. Very similar tasks will show higher correlations, explained on Spearman's theory because they share *s* as well as *g*. For example, we would see a much stronger correlation between two tasks if they both measured Latin vocabulary.) From this pattern of correlations, we can calculate what is called the *g saturation* of each task. This is how strongly performance on the task correlates with *g* itself. In other words, it tells us how well this task measures *g* rather than *s*.

Again, the exact methods do not matter, but the intuition is simple. Some tasks are largely *s* and little *g*—for these tasks, the most important thing is specific ability, with only a weak contribution from *g*. Because a person's score is largely determined by *s*—different from all the *s* factors for other kinds of activity—this task will generally show low correlations with others. In contrast, other tasks are largely *g*, with little contribution from *s*. Because performance on this kind of task is largely determined by *g*, correlation with other things will tend to be higher. Approximately speaking, the *g* saturation for each task in the battery is derived from its average correlation with all the others.

This development of Spearman's reasoning is potentially very important. In practical applications we may wish to know each *person's* *g* score. From the perspective of science, however, what we should really like to know is *what g measures* in terms of underlying psychological or brain functions. Surely, a good clue should be provided by asking what kind of activity depends strongly on *g* and what kind of activity does not.

As it turns out, the "purest" tests of *g* can be very pure indeed. Perhaps the best are problems like the brain teasers you can find in a book of children's puzzles—tests not of knowledge, like vocabulary or arithmetic, but of simple reasoning. The best-known example is a test called Matrices, developed by John Carlyle Raven under Spearman's guidance in the 1930s.[6] The principle is shown in figure 2. At

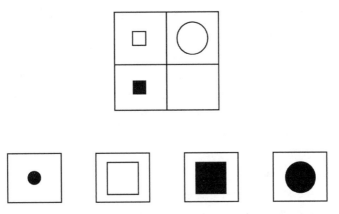

Figure 2. Matrix problem. The task is to decide which of the four choices at the bottom fills in the empty square of the matrix.

the top are four boxes arranged in a two-by-two matrix. Three boxes contain shapes, but the fourth is empty. The task is to decide which shape should go into the empty box and complete the matrix. The possible answers are given in a row at the bottom. The first is right in some ways but not quite perfect. The second is definitely wrong, while the third is closer but still the wrong shape. After some thought, the fourth one is seen to be correct. It has the right shape (a circle), the right size (large), and the right color (black). Such problems can be made very easy or very hard, depending on the rules one uses to construct the matrix. In other brain teaser tests, the subject might be shown a series of shapes and asked to predict which one comes next; or he might be given several groups of four letters and asked to decide which group is the odd one out.

As measured in many experiments, the ability to solve matrix problems has a g saturation around 0.8. In other words, it correlates very well with the g one would obtain by laboriously measuring the average ability to do well on a wide variety of tasks. To me this is another remarkable result. We can measure people's success in a broad variety of activities—either with artificial laboratory tests or using the activities of their real lives. We can combine the results to get an overall estimate of how well this person does things "on the average." But . . . in thirty minutes with Raven's Matrices, we can achieve almost the same result. Somehow, these apparently trivial children's puzzles capture the essence of g. What is it about them that allows this to happen?

At the other extreme, it is easy to find tasks with very low g saturations. Intuitively, these tasks often seem simpler, requiring no real "thought"—pressing a button as quickly as possible when a light flashes, spending two minutes making up as many random designs as possible, recognizing shapes from a few fragments. Other tasks in this category seem to depend strongly on some specific talent (in Spearman's terms, a strong s)—a talent for music, for example.

This brings us back again to our everyday intuitions about "intelligence." Probably most of us would say that solving puzzles seems more "intelligent" than pressing a button as soon as a light comes on. Apparently, this intuition—based presumably on a lifetime's experience of our own mental lives and those of the people around us—has some real relationship to whatever it is that g measures. In terms of true understanding, however, this does not move us very far. In terms of underlying mental or neural processes, how does a task like Raven's Matrices really differ from pressing a button as quickly as possible?

This is an extremely important clue. That said, it is not a clue that is immediately easy to read. The simpler a task is, the easier it seems to analyze it in terms of underlying psychological processes. We have extremely detailed models of how a person accumulates information from the eye and pushes down a finger as soon as a light is detected. These models extend from principles of statistical decision down to detailed brain processes.[7] But the simpler a task is, the less it seems to reflect g—whereas the more complex the task is, the harder it is to know what psychological or brain functions it requires. To read this clue, we shall need to ask what is really so important in "complex" tasks like Raven's Matrices.

Spearman achieved extraordinary things with the abstract concept of g. He was much less detailed on the question we have just been discussing: what it is about the mind that g actually measures.

In *The Abilities of Man*, Spearman proposed that the mind might be seen as a large collection of separate engines, each specialized for a different purpose. This proposal is in line with many specializations of function that we now know for different regions of the brain (discussed in chapter 3). Each engine, Spearman thought, might correspond to a different s. Then he thought that g might reflect something needed by all the engines, like a source of power. In psychological terms, this power might correspond to the amount of attention a person can invest. Certainly we can allocate attention to many different mental activities.

The difficulty is that the actual correlational data do not lend themselves to detailed interpretation in terms of underlying psychological processes. If g does represent a kind of attentional power, why is it measured better by Raven's Matrices than by pressing buttons when lights flash on? We could make up a story (we psychologists can be imaginative), but in truth, there is little in the data that points to this specific theoretical proposal. A century of correlational data repeatedly confirms that g matters. These data are much less clear on what g actually is.

To a psychologist, my discussion of Spearman will seem dated. Since Spearman we have seen a century of work on mental abilities, and few people now think in simple terms of g and s. To my eyes, however, the modern picture is really not that different from what Spearman anticipated. The idea of g in particular has scarcely changed. The big change has been an elaboration on s—and even this is a fairly obvious elaboration, something already directly hinted at in Spearman's 1904 paper.

We said that s is a specific factor (or a set of specific factors) affecting only one kind of activity or task. The s for one task in a battery should be different from the s for other tasks—specifically, they should be uncorrelated, so that a person's value for one s is completely unrelated to his value on all the others. It is as if, when a person is created, they put their hand into a large number of bags, picking out a separate number from each bag. The number picked out of each bag sets the value for one s (with a final bag for the value of g).

But how specific is specific? Put another way, when do two tasks in a battery become so similar that they begin to share things over and above g? This must happen at some time—when we start to think not so much of "two different tasks" but of "two versions of the same task." When does it in fact happen?

Recall that, in his first paper, Spearman devised methods for extracting the common element between different measures of academic achievement and the common element between measures of sensory discrimination. It was a correlation of almost 1 between these common elements that led him to the idea of g. But suppose that we look for common elements between more similar things. The example Spearman calculated was the common element between two different tests of Latin and two different tests of French. This time, his methods did not show a correlation of 1 between the two common elements. Obviously, people who know a lot of Latin—and therefore do well on both Latin tests—need not be the same people who know a lot of French. As Spearman put it: "We can always come upon (specific functions) eventually, if we sufficiently narrow our field of view and consider branches of activity closely enough resembling one another."[8]

With the development of factor analysis, methods became available for examining any number of common elements influencing correlations in a test battery. In the modern picture, abilities are often depicted as a hierarchy.[9] At the bottom are many narrow factors, closely related to Spearman's s factors. The number of these is essentially arbitrary—one can always produce a new specific factor, affecting only a narrow range of tasks, simply by designing more and more very similar task pairs. ("Latin" and "French" do not appear in most modern depictions of the hierarchy, but we could make them appear simply by including several Latin and French tests in our experiments.) There is probably no limit to the number of things in the mind—abilities, learned skills, or just scraps of knowledge—that can affect one tiny area of behavior. At the top of the hierarchy g remains—still resulting from the overall property of positive manifold or universal positive correlation. But in the middle are now added around a dozen so-called group factors—individual abilities that have some influence (not necessarily strong) on a range of the tasks that a modern experiment may include. Such group factors might include a broad ability to do well on verbal tasks, another for spatial tasks, another for memory tasks, another for tasks requiring rapid responses. Again, the exact group factors in any given analysis will be a somewhat accidental consequence of the specific tasks that the experimenter decided to include. In this respect, a central reason that different experiments give reasonably coherent results is that new experimenters tend to copy their predecessors in the tests they use. The general principle, however, is that, over and above g, there can indeed be some "common influences" extending across reasonably broad domains of activity.

Scientists like to believe that they have found something new, and perhaps the most common view of Spearman is that his theory of g and s was ultimately proved wrong by the discovery of group factors. In fact, Spearman realized early on that some influences on behavior would be very narrow, others less so. Specific skills, for example, are extremely narrow. About twenty years ago, I carried out some research to ask what makes a good driver. We took ninety people around a fixed driving route, measuring and recording how they used the controls, where they looked, what safety margins they left, and so on. We found that driving is an extraordinary collection of separate, almost independent skills. For example, a person who conscientiously checks the mirror before slowing down and turning onto a new street may often fail to check the mirror before pulling out to pass—even though any given person does each of these individual things quite consistently. Other influences, though, are inevitably broader in their effects—good command of English, for example. It is actually rather arbitrary to divide these influences into two categories, "specific" and "group." In this respect, my feeling is that Spearman would have seen little to surprise him in the modern hierarchical view. Certainly, he would find little to question his essential idea of g.

There is another dangerous confusion in everyday language (and probably in everyday thinking). Sometimes when we say that a person is intelligent, what we really mean is that they have been well educated. In other words, they know many of the things that we think an "intelligent" person ought to know. How does education relate to g?

In the 1960s, the psychologist Raymond Cattell introduced a distinction between "fluid" and "crystallized" intelligence.[10] Fluid intelligence concerns current ability to solve novel problems. It is typically measured with tasks like Raven's Matrices. Fluid intelligence, accordingly, is very much the same as Spearman's g. Though we may debate their success in this respect, tests like Raven's Matrices were specifically designed for use in different cultures and accordingly tried to minimize dependence on specific education. In contrast, many common IQ tests also use material that is obviously and exclusively the product of a specific culture's education. Tests of vocabulary or arithmetic are cases in point. Cattell called these tests of "crystallized intelligence" or acquired knowledge.

In a normal sample of young people from a similar cultural background, tests of fluid and crystallized intelligence may be strongly correlated. Cattell's idea was that people with high fluid intelligence would tend to learn more from their education. When we measure crystallized intelligence, however, we are not really measuring something about how the person is *now*. We are measuring what he or she was like when the knowledge was learned. Once learned, the knowledge is crystallized—in the sense that, for example, a word once learned is fairly stable and available for the rest of a person's life.

The distinction between fluid and crystallized intelligence is important for several reasons. One is that the two measures can only show high correlation if educational or cultural opportunities are fairly constant across the population examined. If opportunities vary—which in fact they always will—differences in crystallized achievements will partly arise through different opportunities to acquire the knowledge that is tested. It is easy to see that English vocabulary will not show much correlation with Raven's Matrices if half the people we test are English and half are French. Arguably, however, this is just what we do if we test for vocabulary that is only widely used in some parts of a culture.

For our purposes, there is something even more important. As a measure of current ability, fluid intelligence is very sensitive to change. The most common change—since it happens to everybody— is change with age. From about the mid-teens—and certainly from the twenties onward—our fluid intelligence begins to decline. The same person can solve fewer and fewer problems in Raven's Matrices, until by our seventies, few of us can match even the average young person. Obviously, there is no parallel decline in such things as vocabulary. Though it may take longer to bring them to mind, the number of words a person knows does not change much as he or she ages. In this respect, we may all be grateful for crystallization. It follows that, if an experiment includes both young and old people, fluid and crystallized tests will show little correlation. As age progresses, the two pull farther and farther apart.

What applies to age applies with equal force to brain damage. (This should not surprise us, since accumulating cell damage lies at the heart of declining ability in old age.) To understand the effects of damage to different parts of the brain, we must distinguish carefully between fluid and crystallized tests. Vocabulary, for example, is sensitive to brain damage in a way that is quite different from Raven's Matrices. In the next chapters we will see how things go wrong if the distinction between fluid and crystallized intelligence is ignored.

It will be obvious by now that I greatly admire what Spearman did. I would place both his results and his conclusions among the most imaginative and solid achievements of experimental psychology. At the same time, few ideas have generated so much uneasiness, denial, and downright dislike. In our competitive world, we have every reason for concern over people's achievements. When we think about the theory of g, however, we must keep a clear hold on what it does and does not say—as well as what it does and does not mean for how we conduct our lives.

One common reaction is this: Surely people's nature cannot be reduced to just one number, the score they obtain on an IQ test? Surely their worth cannot be captured in one number? Each person is a unique constellation of many things—countless special talents, a reservoir of personal knowledge and experience built through an individual lifetime, a personality of uncountable facets and shades. By reducing such wealth to a single number, doesn't g miss out on the true variety and fascination of human nature?

I have often heard people attack the idea that a person can be reduced to just one number. I don't think, though, that I have ever heard anybody defend it. Obviously, nothing like this is implied by Spearman's theory of g and s factors. In the concept of g, the theory proposes one thing about human nature. A large body of work shows that this thing is important. But the theory also admits an infinite number of other things, also important in different ways. Certainly it is not reasonable to expect any scientific theory to deal simultaneously with everything.

As for worth, this is simply outside the realm of Spearman's theory. We value the people we meet for countless things, for their integrity, their laughter, their decency, their dignity, their charm, their coolness, their loyalty. We admire ski jumpers, artists, those who fight oppression, those who protect others, those who will not give in, those who can raise the concerns of others above their own. We value and love people for uncountable different things . . . but this is not what Spearman's theory is about. It is about one extraordinary observation concerning human behavior and how we might explain that observation.

A similar line of thought is reflected in the frequent definition of new kinds of "intelligence": practical intelligence, social intelligence, emotional intelligence. As we have known from Spearman onward (in fact, we hardly need science to show us this), people vary in countless ways, and somehow it seems fair to capture this by defining many varieties of "intelligence." In fact, as I explained earlier, the word "intelligence" itself has little definite meaning. If we wish, we are at liberty to call just a few things "intelligence," or many different things. It is certain that human nature and ability have infinite variations; their importance is not affected by what we call them.

A second reaction is that g implies a fate hanging over us no matter what efforts we put in. I began this chapter with my friend's remark that "everybody in America would hate me," and in fact, I do think that the idea of g threatens a basic belief of Americans in particular. This belief is that the world is filled with opportunity and that people who try will get ahead. It is a small step—but again, a non sequitur—to believe that opportunities are equal for everybody and that hard work is all that matters.

I firmly agree with the first idea. What I most love about American culture is the belief that putting your back into something is worth it. I am constantly ashamed of my British tendency to shrug, grin, and think that perhaps something is not worth the bother. However, I think it is untrue—as well as unfair—to suppose that everybody's chances are the same and that all people's efforts will be repaid by similar rewards. For any given person, it is certainly best to try hard, but this does not mean that all people who try hard will achieve the same result. We do live in a world where each person's unique potential can be turned to its best advantage. Obviously, we do not live in a world where all abilities are the same, and in this respect, Spearman's g is merely one salient case in point.

A third concern is that the idea of g contributes to social division—to racism, sexism, class discrimination. It is commonly found, for example, that IQ distributions are different in different racial groups. Of course, this does not tell us anything about individuals; it concerns only the spread of scores in large groups. Especially in the United States, enormous debate has attached to these findings and their potential political implications. Although there are vital psychological and political concerns in this debate, in my view, these concerns should be about prejudice, not about g.

As a simple fact, a difference in IQ distributions between racial groups strikes me, at best, as a scientific curiosity. The facts are not surprising; considered as whole groups rather than as individuals, for example, American blacks and whites have different genes, different incomes, different schooling, and different lives, and considering all of this, it would be remarkable if IQ distributions (or any other distributions) turned out to be just the same. Neither, in my view, are the facts especially interesting, in the sense that they pose an urgent scientific problem or one likely to be informatively solved. With so many uncontrollable factors potentially affecting the IQ distributions of different groups, it is hard to imagine that definite explanations will ever be easy to come by.

Meanwhile, absorption in the facts can easily distract us from real political concerns. For example, a long-running debate surrounds the question of whether genetic factors contribute to racial differences. Both politically and scientifically, this debate seems to me to be largely beside the point: a problem not easy to solve, concerned with whole distributions rather than individuals, at best, as I say, a curiosity. Meanwhile, what is absolutely beyond debate is the influence of environment. We hardly need science to tell us that life and achievements are shaped by opportunity: in education, resources, the influence of parents and peers. In our societies, furthermore, we know that these opportunities are not at all equal across either individuals or groups. Politically speaking, these inequalities of opportunity are something that really matters—something unfair in our society, something shaping the lives of millions of citizens, and something (unlike genes) we could actually, with enough willpower, address. This is what racism is really about, not about abstract group differences, but about according individual people different opportunities, rights, value, and respect.

This is not to say that science has no place in this kind of political arena. Though facts themselves cannot be racist, they can contribute to racism. A large and fascinating research literature in social psychology documents the strong human tendency to form groups of "us" and "them" at every level from family to classroom to football team supporter to nation. It shows how we accord rights and value to "us" and often denigrate or distrust "them," whether "they" are whites, women, Muslims, or children living in a different bunkhouse.[11] This feature of our thinking is so strong that I doubt any of us fully avoids it; perhaps the best we can do is to be vigilant for its appearance and to remember how misleading and irrational it is likely to be. Perhaps this is the real reason for such concern with racial differences in IQ: not that any facts in themselves have much intrinsic interest, but that they feed into our human absorption with "us" and "them" groups. In my opinion, science might indeed have much to contribute to real issues of political thought and action; but this science should concern the psychology of discrimination and prejudice, not the psychology of g.

The abuse of knowledge in discrimination and prejudice leads to a final non sequitur that is often raised against work on a brain basis for g. As long as g is just an abstraction, the thought runs, perhaps it remains somehow less real? Might we fear that a physical basis in the brain makes the idea stronger and in this way more open to abuse? Plausible though this sounds, it really makes no sense—especially not for a psychologist, a person concerned with the facts and explanation of human behavior. However it is explained, g concerns behavior. It is defined by what people *do*. If g is defined in behavior, it has some basis in the brain, but certainly this is not the source of its importance. It is the *behavior itself* that matters—we care about g because of its relevance to people's actions and hence their lives, and we would care just the same whether its physical basis lay in the brain or the heart. Facts of behavior may be explained by events in the brain, but the explanation in no way changes those facts.

On the whole, in fact, I think it may be *easier*, not harder, to misuse an ill-defined idea of "intelligence" than to misuse the well-defined idea of g. A poorly defined idea is malleable and for this reason can be used to extract all sorts of potential implications. This is much harder with something well-defined and concrete. The better we understand something, the more clearly we can think about it. The better we understand g, the easier it may be to restrict what we think it implies.

We can examine the science of g and its origin in basic cognitive and brain mechanisms. We can argue about political choices and the distribution of opportunity in our society. We can examine our human values and the things we respect or admire. It is useful to remember, though, that serious non sequiturs are needed to move among these different things. Later I shall discuss our human tendency to reason in rather loose clouds of only apparently related ideas. To avoid this trap, "the science and politics of IQ" must be kept carefully apart.[12]

Now it is time to return to our story. As this chapter has considered in detail, g concerns differences between one person and another. These differences are interesting, and Spearman's work in unraveling them is spectacular. Behind them, however, lies a rather bigger idea. The most crucial idea is not that one person has high g and another low. The most crucial idea is that something could exist in the mind to make this possible.

A key difficulty in experimental psychology is knowing which way to turn. Faced with the infinite diversity of human activity, we badly need signposts hinting which parts of the jungle to explore. If Spearman's theory is correct, this suggests something basic and important—some underlying quality or mental process that exerts a major influence on a great many things we do. If something like

g exists, it points to something important in everybody. This is the really big idea for science to engage with.

The work I have described in this chapter also gives us a very specific lead. This lead comes from the best tests of g and their extraordinary ability to measure something significant. With fluid intelligence tests—simple puzzles like Raven's Matrices—we approach the heart of something essential in the human mind. What is so special about puzzles like these? What do they tell us of our minds and brains?

Spearman's idea of g was derived from measurements of human behavior. It was an abstract idea proposed to explain how positive manifold arises.

But if g exists, it must also be concrete. As behavior derives from the brain, so must g be produced by the brain. In some way or other, something in brain function must explain what g is.

Chapter 3 **Inside**

In chapter 1, I discussed how strange it is to adopt the psychologist's perspective—to look at ourselves, not from the inside out, but from the outside in. This becomes even stranger when we look right inside the box and consider that somehow the selves we know emerge from a soft bodily organ. It is somehow hard to believe that the mind is created by the biological tissue of the brain.

Yet, soft, fatty, honeycombed with tiny blood vessels, this at the same time is the person who admires the sunset, writes a novel, or is enraptured by a baby. In this chapter I introduce the basics of brain anatomy and function—what structures the brain contains, the nerve cells these structures are built from, and how networks of many millions of these cells make mind and behavior happen.

Obviously, all of our thought and behavior is produced and controlled by our brains. Indeed, a moment's thought shows that the only reason animals have brains or minds at all is to control the actions that help them to survive. Since the second half of the twentieth century, it has been popular to think of the brain as a kind of computer—biological, complex, and powerful, but a kind of computer nevertheless.

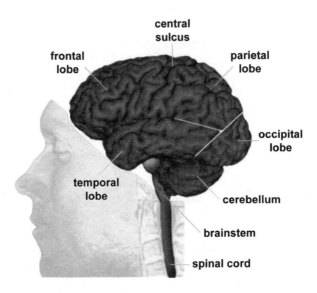

Figure 3. The human brain viewed from the left.

This, too, can seem unsettling, but is perhaps less radical than it seems. The idea is simply that, like a computer, the brain takes up information—analyzes it, integrates it, stores it—and ultimately uses it in control of action.

The broad structure of the human brain is shown in figure 3. The full "central nervous system" consists of the brain and spinal cord; here, just the top part of the spinal cord is shown. The brain, enclosed in the skull, is joined to the top of the spinal cord. Below this, the spinal cord extends all the way down the back to where the spine ends.

The spinal cord receives sensations of touch, position, pain, and so on from the surface of the body. It sends back instructions to the muscles, allowing the body to be moved. Even at this primitive level there is a fascinating ability to generate organized, useful behavior. Even when it is disconnected from the brain, for example, the spinal cord of a cat can control such activities as pulling the paw back from water and shaking it off or elementary forms of standing and stepping. Of course, the spinal cord does not act in a vacuum. It is constantly receiving instructions of many kinds from higher levels. Even on its own, though, it can control some very complicated activities.

Above the spinal cord we enter a succession of brain levels, increasing in complexity. The same basic pattern exists in almost all vertebrates, though with increasing complexity of the higher brain levels as we move from fish to birds and mammals. The most primitive level, the brain stem, controls such elementary bodily functions as respiration and heartbeat. It is important in sleep and wakefulness. As you might expect for a structure connected to the spinal cord, many parts of the brain stem are also concerned with movement. At the top of the brain stem is the midbrain—already well developed in an amphibian such as a frog. For example, it contains a structure called the optic tectum, receiving information from the eye and allowing the frog to analyze the contents of the visual world. This visual information can be used to guide all sorts of actions, such as snapping at a fly or escaping from a predator.

At the back of the brain sits the cerebellum, a slightly mysterious structure. Certainly, the cerebellum has important motor functions. (In physiology, "motor" means concerned with movement, while "sensory" means concerned with information from the senses.) A patient with cerebellar damage will have characteristic motor difficulties, in particular a striking tremor or shaking that is added onto any movement that is attempted. At the same time, it increasingly seems that there is much more to the human cerebellum than movement. Unfortunately, this is not well understood; in this book there will be little of the cerebellum.

At the top of the complexity hierarchy, we come to the cerebral cortex. In figure 3 this is the large structure at the top. The cerebral cortex has evolved on top of preexisting structures and has accordingly been built to work along with them. For example, the motor systems in the cerebral cortex must send commands to the spinal cord and must operate in terms of the organization and structure already existing there. They must also operate in concert with the cerebellum, which is also interacting with the spinal cord. Similarly, the cerebral cortex contains a complex visual system, analyzing many aspects of the visual world. It, too, must deal with such preexisting structures as the optic tectum, which also analyzes visual information and its implications for action. The cerebral cortex is essential to much of what we would call mental or cognitive life. For example, when a stroke destroys a person's language, it is the cerebral cortex that has been damaged.

The cerebral cortex consists of two similar hemispheres, left and right, joined across the middle. Conventionally, each hemisphere is divided into four "lobes"—occipital, parietal, temporal and frontal—though these divisions are rather arbitrary, the names actually coming from the overlying bones of the skull. More interesting are the *functional* divisions, which part of the cortex does what. The picture in figure 3 will be a useful road map as the story of this book unfolds. With this map in mind we can turn from anatomy to function—to how it is that brain tissue works.

The basic building block of the brain is the nerve cell or neuron. In the human brain there are perhaps ten billion to a thousand billion neurons. This means that, if a brain was divided into ten thousand tiny pieces, each of these might still contain about a hundred million neurons. The communication of information among these neurons underlies everything the brain can do.

Each neuron is essentially an information integrator. At its input end are connections from a great many other neurons. A typical figure for just one neuron in the brain might be ten thousand of these connections. Each connection exerts a tiny influence on the activity of the cell. With the right input from these thousands of connections, the cell "fires." It sends out an electrical impulse to all those other cells that, in turn, receive connections from it. The brain is thus a vast web of information integrators, each one waiting until it sees some particular combination of inputs from other cells, then sending the information that this combination occurred along to thousands of others.

Tiny though they are, the impulses of a single neuron can be recorded with a microelectrode, inserted into the brain to record electrical activity in one small area of tissue. In a typical experiment, the electrode will pick up activity from just one or a few neurons. With experiments of this sort, we see how neurons work and what makes them fire.

As you might imagine, a great deal of the communication in the brain is quite local. Cells get much of their information from other cells close by and send much of it back over a similar short distance. It is not all this way, however. Incredibly for such tiny entities, cells also send information across many centimeters. The nerve impulse travels along a tiny output wire (the axon) growing out from the body of the cell. (It does not actually work like electrical transmission along a wire—it is much slower—but still, it takes just a fraction of a second for the message to arrive.) Whole bundles of axons/wires travel from one part of the brain to another; for example, one such bundle travels all the way from the occipital lobe (at the back of the brain) to the frontal lobe (at the front). In the spinal cord there are cells with even longer axons. Our muscles contract and move our bodies because they receive instructions (impulses) from neurons telling them to do so. The cell bodies of these neurons are in the spinal cord, so to reach a muscle in the foot, an axon must extend up to a meter or more.

How can these webs of neurons operate, taking up useful information from the world and turning it into useful behavior? To explain the principle, we can go back to the ethologists' idea of the innate releasing mechanism and how sequences of IRMs create behavior that is coordinated and effective. When a toad sees a worm, it responds with a characteristic series of movements. It turns toward the worm, approaches, fixes its head in position, and snaps. What neural network can make this happen? Neurophysiologists have examined this question in great detail, and though much remains uncertain, the results give a fascinating general picture of how neural networks operate.[1]

First, the toad needs to know that a worm is there. In the eye of the toad—as in the eye of any other animal—there are special neurons that respond to different patterns of light. Specifically, each neuron fires for a particular patch, falling onto a particular part of the eye and moving in a particular way. How you would construct these patch detectors is a problem in itself, but for the moment we can take them as a given. This visual patchwork makes up the basic information that the toad's brain has to work with.

Neurons in the eye send impulses to several brain regions. For catching prey, the most important is the optic tectum in the midbrain. Like the eye itself, the optic tectum is laid out like a map, corresponding to the area of space that the toad can see. Information from different parts of the eye goes to different places on the map. The map is involved in all sorts of visual behavior, not just snapping at worms. Correspondingly, the information it receives must be analyzed in many ways.

A worm is long, thin, and reasonably small, and it tends to move in the direction of its long axis. All these properties are important—for example, a toad will snap at a long, thin bar moving in the correct direction but not at the same bar moving sideways in a way that a worm never would. Already we can see why a neuron needs to combine information from multiple sources in deciding what output it should give. Somehow, cells in the optic tectum must put together just the right patch information to determine that a worm is there—that the combination of moving patches it sees is the combination a worm would produce. Exactly how cells achieve this is not at all certain, but we do know that, somewhere in the optic tectum, the problem is solved. Recording with microelectrodes, we can find cells that do exactly what they should: respond only to long, thin stripes moving in the direction of the long axis.

Now the toad knows a worm is there, but it still needs to decide what to do. The optic tectum transmits information to motor structures in the lower brain stem and spinal cord. These motor structures can actually send out the commands for actions such as turning the body, approaching, fixating and snapping. (Again, it is a complex question how a neural network could actually coordinate such actions as snapping and swallowing, but again, we are taking this complex part of the problem as a given.) More information is needed, however, to decide what the right motor command should be. If the worm is off to one side, this will be indicated by where on the eye its image falls and thus where in the map it is detected. Now the correct action is to turn toward it. If it is ahead but far away, the correct action is to approach. (And it is not easy to determine whether an object is close by or far away. Whereas the image on the eye is two-dimensional, the world it reflects is three-dimensional. This means that a similar pattern of light arriving at the eye could have come from a small object close by or a much larger object farther off. There are many tricks that vision can employ to calculate depth or distance—but implementing these tricks is much more work, involving additional information integration.) Only when the worm is close by and straight ahead is the correct action at last to snap.

Already the problem is seeming quite complicated, but with a little more thought we can see how much more will be needed before this simple scheme can work. For example, now think about a frog instead of a toad, shooting out its sticky tongue to snap up a fly. Sticky tongue or no, a fly is not an easy thing to catch. In fact, snapping at the place where the fly was detected is not going to be any use; by the time the information has passed through the brain and the muscles have contracted, the fly will be gone. Obviously, we are going to need something that locates the fly's current position—and its speed and direction of movement—then sends just the right snap to arrive at the right place at the right time. This sort of prediction must be a constant feature of a great many neural networks, anticipating and correcting for the effects of movement in our own bodies and the world around us.

Going back to the toad, new problems arise when the head turns on the body. (The problem would be even more complex if the toad, like us, could also scan the world by swiveling its eyes in its head.) When the toad sees a worm to one side, the body should be turned toward that side. But how much should it turn? For a worm seen on a particular part of the eye, the amount of turn will depend on the angle between the head and the rest of the body. Somehow, the registration between visual maps and motor commands must use additional signals informing the toad of the current position of its head.

We could go on like this for a while. The toad is much more likely to snap when it is hungry than when it is full. More integration of different kinds of information. It does not snap at all if, at the same moment as the worm appears, a looming figure approaches. Now, instead, the toad freezes and begins to puff up. More integration of the many sensory inputs that the toad simultaneously receives.

This example shows both how much and how little we know of brain function. On the one hand, this is a fascinating glimpse of how millions of tiny cells can direct an animal's capture of its prey. On the other, even for this relatively simple case of the toad and the worm, many problems are entirely unsolved. Certainly, we could not even begin to build an artificial neural network that could mimic the real complexities of the toad's behavior.

For most problems beyond the toad and worm, we know even less, though we have many useful-seeming fragments. We do understand, however, that these are the general principles of brain operation—neurons combining multiple sources of information to work out useful facts about the world and using those facts to direct effective pieces of behavior.

As we consider more complex mental activity, many obvious questions arise. For example, how does a neural network learn? Let us suppose that, in your own visual system, a cluster of neurons has combined enough visual information to determine that a visible object is a silver ball in the night sky. Somehow, this cluster must learn to connect to patterns of neurons elsewhere in the brain—neurons controlling speech movements—so that, when you want to talk about that object, you know to say "moon." This idea of experience-dependent connection is basic to learning in neural networks. Much research asks when, where, and how it is produced.[2]

Another important topic is selective attention. As discussed in chapter 1 in the experiments with speech messages, a person in a crowded room can listen either to one conversation or to another. Both conversations arrive at the ear; it seems as though, depending on the context, different patterns of neural connections are enabled or closed off. Indeed, many experiments show something just like this in neurons of the monkey visual system—when the animal pays attention to one object, that object controls neural firing, but when attention moves to something new, the old firing pattern disappears, and a new pattern reflecting the properties of the new object takes its place.[3]

In principle, indeed, we would like to understand *all* mental life in terms of the operation of neural networks. From the perspective of the physiologist, neural networks are the basic mechanism explaining all that we know and do: how we feel disgust at the sight of rotten food, how we understand and feel for others, how we reach out and pick up a beer glass, how we plan a holiday to Italy and later remember the food and architecture.

Now we have seen the crude structure of the brain and how each part of this structure is a complex neural network receiving, transforming, and sending out information. A natural thought is: Surely we can understand this system by splitting it into parts and discovering what each separate part does? This thought is perhaps the main conceptual cornerstone of modern experimental psychology and brain science. It has produced conspicuous successes.

Not surprisingly, the simplest brain functions are easiest to understand. In the human cerebral cortex (and brains of other mammals such as cats and monkeys), visual information arrives from the eye right at the back, in the occipital lobe. (Figure 3 will be useful again here.) The first parts of the system form maps like the one I discussed in the toad, and neurons in these maps establish relatively simple properties of the visual world. Where are edges seen between dark and light? What wavelength (color) of light is coming from each region? This information is then distributed to a whole set of adjacent regions, extending through the occipital lobe and into parts of parietal and temporal lobes. In each region visual information is used to address further questions. Are objects moving, or does the image move on the eye because the eye has moved itself? What shape does an object have (a ball, a cup, a friend's face)? Where are objects positioned, and what movements would be needed to look at them or to reach out and pick them up?

For other senses there are equivalent cortical regions. Information from the ears, for example, arrives in a part of the temporal lobe and is distributed to a network of regions extracting different varieties of auditory information. Information from the body surface arrives at the front edge of the parietal lobe. This information is also needed for many things: to identify objects by touch, to feel vibration or tickle, and very important, to keep track of where all the parts of the body are, essential for controlling movement. This close functional correspondence between body sense and movement is reflected in anatomical proximity. Just across a fissure (the central sulcus) dividing the parietal and frontal lobes, we move into motor areas of the brain. The "primary motor cortex," immediately in front of the central sulcus, contains cells whose firing quite directly instructs particular fragments of movement, such as a twitch of one finger. Moving forward into the frontal lobe, neurons come to be concerned with more complex, higher-order movement patterns—very much as, further back in the brain, successive levels of sensory processing extract more and more complex properties of the sensory world.

Can this "divide-and-conquer" strategy be continued indefinitely, into more and more abstract aspects of cognition and mind? Can the full complexity of our mental life be divided into "modules," separate functions carried out by discrete regions of the brain? It is an attractive idea and one that can be examined using a range of neuroscientific and psychological methods.

One very direct method is the study of brain damage or, as it is called in medicine, brain lesion. When a person suffers a stroke or a head injury or has a brain tumor removed, there will often be damage to one quite restricted part of the brain. If this part of the brain has some specific cognitive function, this function should be evident in how the person's behavior is changed.

Since the nineteenth century, this method has given some of our clearest views of brain modules. For example, it shows that, in most human beings, language is a left hemisphere function. After left hemisphere lesion, especially lesion to the back of the frontal lobe or to the junction of temporal and parietal lobes, language problems ("aphasias") are common. In contrast, little usually happens to language when the right hemisphere is damaged. Another well-known example is "amnesia," or the inability to store new information in memory. An amnesic patient may be quite normal in his or her immediate interactions with the surrounding world. For example, the patient may be quite able to look up a telephone number, remember it, and successfully dial it. Little or nothing sticks, though, in longer-term memory. The patient may be quite unable to remember what memory tests were carried out an hour previously or that the same psychologist has visited on several previous occasions. Amnesia is most commonly seen after damage to a specific, closely connected set of regions on the inner surface of the temporal lobe (the surface buried in the middle of the brain).

Taking this kind of work further, neuropsychology (as this enterprise is called) has defined many kinds of impairment after brain damage. Many of these impairments are astonishingly specific. For example, a patient may be good at reading written words but unable to identify faces—suggesting that, somewhere in the visual system, there is a face module or at least a set of visual processes that are much more important for faces than for words. A patient may be able to imitate movements but unable to make them spontaneously on command (even though the words of the command are certainly understood). In "deep dyslexia," the patient can read such concrete words as "chair" or "bucket" but not the simplest function words, such as "and," "if," or "but." (Fascinatingly, these same patients often show a bizarre error called "semantic"—reading a word, not as itself, and not as a word that looks similar, but as a word related in *meaning*. For example, the patient might read "table" as "chair," or "gun" as "cannon.") The list is apparently endless. Sometimes it seems that each microscopic scrap of our mental lives is separately controlled in the brain and thus separately sensitive to damage.

Again there is something unsettling here. If we are jumbles of many separate parts, then where is the "person"? The integrated "self"? In neuropsychology it is common to face this dilemma, to see single people apparently divided by the results of their brain damage.

A good case in point is a patient, DF, made famous by the studies of David Milner and Mel Goodale.[4] DF was poisoned by carbon monoxide, released by a faulty water heater while she was showering. The result was massive brain damage, in particular affecting large areas of both occipital lobes. As expected, occipital damage was associated with major visual difficulties: DF could no longer copy or identify drawings, reliably read words or recognize faces, or decide whether two objects were the same or different. In many respects, you would say that DF was blind . . . but DF's body was not. Suppose you showed her a large disc with a slot cut in it. She could tell you nothing about the orientation of this slot. She could not describe it or copy it by turning another disc until its slot was at the same angle. But if you gave her a card and asked her to place it through the slot, then suddenly she reached out and obeyed, turning the card to just the right angle as her hand moved. When visual information reaches the brain, its processing is split into several pathways. One goes down from the occipital into the temporal lobe. This pathway is important in identifying the objects around us and is perhaps used when we describe what things we see. A second pathway runs from the occipital up to the parietal lobe, to regions involved in the planning and control of movements. In DF, it seems that the same visual information reached bodily control but not conscious perception; it could direct the hand but not conscious experience.

Something similar is seen in the much more frequent condition of unilateral neglect. In the brain, the representation of the world is largely crossed—to a large extent, the right cerebral hemisphere is concerned with events to the person's left, while the left cerebral hemisphere is concerned with events to the right. (This is a very oversimplified description, but enough for the moment.) When one side of the brain is damaged, especially through a sudden stroke, there is often a period of "neglect" for the opposite side of space. If the damage is on the left, the person may behave as though events to the right do not exist; even more commonly, if the damage is to the right, the left side is ignored.

Apparently, the patient has lost all awareness of events on the neglected side. He or she may leave food on one side of the plate, shave just one half of the face, or ignore questions asked by a person standing on the neglected side. In controlled experiments, the patient may be quite unable to guess whether objects are present or absent on that side. Yet some parts of the person can know, not only that something was there, but exactly what it was. Suppose that the object is a picture. Half a second after it flashes up, the person sees some-thing else—a string of letters presented at the center of gaze, where it can be seen perfectly well. The person is asked to press a button as quickly as possible to say whether this string of letters is a familiar word. A normal person is somewhat faster if the word matches the preceding picture or is similar in meaning. The brain finds it slightly easier to decide that "dog" is a word if it just saw a picture of a cat. This holds for a normal person, and sometimes it still holds for the patient, even though the picture is flashed on the neglected side. In some sense the patient saw nothing—he or she may not even know that the picture was there and certainly cannot say what it was, but

somebody in the head knows, and if the picture was cat, that somebody can still speed up the recognition of "dog."[5]

Since the late 1980s, this work with patients has been supplemented with a new method: functional brain imaging. In the 1970s,
new techniques had begun to provide detailed structural images of
the human brain—initially using X-rays (the CT scan), later magnetic resonance imaging (MRI). These methods showed the physical
structure of a person's brain—for example, whether it was normal or
showed shrinkage caused by old age. Shortly after, work was begun
on analogous methods for functional imaging. These methods show
not physical structure but what the brain is doing. Nowadays, the
most commonly used method also depends on magnetic resonance
imaging; it is called functional MRI. When a part of the brain works,
it uses oxygen and calls for more blood. The resulting changes can be
picked up with MRI—not directly measuring neural activity, which
is what we are interested in, but the changes in blood supply that
follow. With this method, we can ask again about modularity—what
parts of the brain work when a person speaks, sees a face, or stores
something in memory. Results now come from many thousands of
experiments. Often, earlier results from patients or from animal experiments are confirmed or dramatically amplified. For example, in
the human occipital lobe we now see a whole network of higher-level
"visual areas," very much like those that were already known from
microelectrode experiments in cats and monkeys. We find regions
of the human visual system that appear highly dedicated to processing particular sorts of input—for example, regions that mainly seem
to process faces and others that work out the general layout of a
visual scene.[6] Functional MRI experiments also reveal many properties of brain activity that could not possibly have been anticipated
from work with patients or animals. For the first time, we have a

practical method for detailed, systematic dissection of human brain activity.

In other attempts to divide mental life into separate functional components, there is no direct reference to the brain. One method returns to the problems of divided attention that we discussed in chapter 1. Think again of the air-traffic controller listening to several simultaneous messages coming from different planes. In the 1950s, when people first took an interest in problems of this sort, they supposed there must be some very general limit on the amount of information that the brain could process at one time.[7] If the brain was analyzing the content of one message, it could not deal at the same time with another—corresponding to our everyday experience that focusing attention on one thing means little awareness of others. Soon, however, this theory of a single processing limit had to be revised. As it turns out, our ability to do several things at once depends strongly on how similar they are. This effect of similarity does not sit well with the idea of a single limit.

Imagine again that a person is hearing two streams of words, one arriving at the left ear, and the other at the right. We already know that he will have great trouble listening to both at once, and his difficulty can be shown experimentally by any measure of how much he has heard. For example, the words in each ear may be mainly numbers, with occasional letters. If we ask the subject to press a button every time he hears a letter in either message, many of these targets may be missed. The experiment can also be run with visual rather than auditory stimuli. This time we ask the person to pay attention to two separate streams of visual events. To mimic the auditory experiment, we might ask the person to keep his eyes fixed on a point in the center of a computer screen. Then one series of numbers (with occasional letters) flashes up, one after the other, just to the left of this point, and another flashes up just to the right. The subject is asked to pay attention to both streams, again looking out for letter targets, and again many of these may be missed. The key result is obtained in the last part of this experiment. This time, we do not ask our subject to pay attention to two auditory streams or to two visual streams. Instead, we ask him to monitor *one of each*—maybe an auditory stream presented to the left ear, and a visual stream presented just to the right of the point he is staring at. Suddenly, this is much easier.[8] Our general limit on processing simultaneous streams of information has been replaced by a much greater ability, *as long as these streams come in different sensory modalities.*

We already saw that, at least in the early stages, information from different sensory modalities is processed in separate areas of the brain. It is now tempting to think that, at least to some degree, these different processing systems have their *own individual* "attentional" limits—their own limits on how much they can process at once. More generally, it is often true that divided attention is easier if the things to be done are dissimilar. It is easier if the mental content is rather different—for example, if one task is verbal and the other is spatial. It is easier if the responses are different—for example, if one is spoken and the other is manual. Just as we saw in neuropsychological and functional MRI experiments, we move toward a view of multiple mental modules, each doing somewhat separate things and each with its own limit on how much it can do at one time.

The divide-and-conquer strategy is enormously important. I have given only a sample of its many successes, and on any grounds, we cannot imagine understanding an organ as complex as the brain without recognizing its separation into parts. Still, this approach leaves central questions unanswered. At any given time, we are not a visual system working on one problem, an auditory system on another, a language system on a third, and a memory system on a fourth. Somehow, all these parts of the mind and brain must be integrated—typically working together on one momentary, coherent line of thought and action. This is not to deny what we have already seen of the possibility for parallel processing—for different systems to work at least to some degree on separate, unrelated things. Still, in normal life this is perhaps not the rule. Instead, we find ourselves pursuing some specific set of current goals or concerns—taking up relevant information from multiple sensory modalities, retrieving relevant information from long-term memory, experiencing related emotional reactions, making relevant movements of eyes, hands, vocal tract. We can try to understand all this by splitting the problem into bits, but only if we remember that at some time these bits will need reassembling.

Now it is time to return to *g*. In this chapter we have seen a mind composed of many separate modules. In many cases, separate parts of the brain have their own specific functions—visual object recognition, speech comprehension, navigation, detailed movements of eyes or hand. At the same time, our mental lives are in general coherent. Separate parts must be integrated and work together. How might the idea of *g* fit into this picture? How does *g* match the modular mind?

Chapter 4 **Making the Link**

n some ways, Spearman's ideas map well onto the modular mind and brain. Recall that, for each task we might undertake, Spearman proposed two kinds of contribution. First is the g factor, a general ability to do many things well. Second are the s factors, the individual skills, knowledge, aptitudes that bear on specific activities. In any particular task, the two factors combine to determine the overall level of performance.

Evidently, the s factors sound a lot like the modules we might see from neuropsychology or functional brain imaging using MRI. Just as we see after brain damage, Spearman's theory proposed innumerable separate s factors: s factors that might be specific, perhaps, for recognizing faces or reading words from a certain grammatical class or controlling movements of the hand. If specialized brain modules vary in efficiency from one person to the next, the result will be the s factors of Spearman's theory. As discussed in chapter 2, the s factors must also be supplemented by such group factors as broad "verbal" or "spatial" ability. Again it is easy to see how these somewhat broader abilities might map onto mind or brain modules, such as the language system of the left hemisphere.

But where does this line of thinking leave g? How will we relate the modular view—supported as it is by overwhelming evidence—to the idea of some universal g factor—some factor affecting success in all manner of activities? There are two possibilities, one crude and one subtle. The crude one follows Spearman and looks for a specific cognitive or brain process that corresponds to g. In this chapter I develop this crude alternative, which as it turns out I favor. First, though, let me explain the subtle one.

Spearman's major experimental discovery—the phenomenon of positive manifold, meaning positive correlations between all tasks—is more or less universally accepted. There is no real question over the basic facts. The concept of g, however, is only one possible explanation for those facts. Early on, a different explanation was suggested by a man who became Spearman's great rival, Sir Godfrey Thomson.[1] This explanation is transparently consistent with a modular mind—in fact, it depends on it. Once you have seen this possibility, it seems so inevitable, so elegant, that it simply must be correct.

Suppose there is no g. Instead, the mind is composed of some unknown large number of separate parts or functions. Today we might call them modules; predating modern thinking by almost a century, Thomson called them "bonds." These bonds are all separate and independent—varying independently in strength or efficiency from one person to another. Translating this theory into Spearman's terms, we might say that there are only s factors, without g.

Any task will depend on a subset of the mind's bonds. For example, deciding whether a patch of dots moved left or right (one of the simplest tasks that a psychologist might study) will depend on bonds (think "modules") that concern visual perception, bonds for choosing and making the right response, perhaps bonds for keeping attention focused on the task at hand, and so on. An auditory task may depend on some of the same bonds but will certainly need different ones, too. Essentially, each task calls up its own, somewhat random subset of bonds, and overall task performance depends on the joint strengths of all the bonds involved.

Perhaps it is already clear that this model predicts positive manifold. Any two tasks are perhaps likely to share at least a few bonds. (This assumes that the number of bonds in a single task is some significant proportion of the total.) So they will have at least some positive correlation. When tasks share many bonds, the correlation may be quite high. With this model, however, there is no reason to predict negative correlations. The prediction—just as the facts show—is a set of only positive correlations, ranging from very low to reasonably high.

On this model, a person will still have an overall or average ability to do things well. This average ability can still be measured using Spearman's methods. But what this average ability reflects is now just the average efficiency of all a person's bonds. Because they are most representative, the best tests of average ability will be those that sample or depend on as many bonds as possible. However, the apparent g measured by these tests is just an average of many independent things; there is no true g factor. On this model, g is a statistical abstraction, with no correspondence in a particular cognitive process—and certainly no correspondence in a particular function of the brain.

The elegance of this model comes from its sense of inevitability. In itself, the model is constructed from the most general principles, with no specific g built in. Nevertheless, something that looks just like a g comes out.

So now we have two quite different explanations—Spearman's and Thomson's—both able to handle the same data. Thomson spent a lifetime showing how his model could mimic Spearman's. A century of correlational studies has not adjudicated between the two. Indeed, I think it is fair to say that correlational data alone cannot do this.

I said, though, that I have my own preference for Spearman. Why? Why prefer the crude explanation—that a g is specifically built in— to the subtle one—that it emerges inevitably from the statistics of building complex tasks out of simple components?

Remember that there are two ways to obtain a good measure of g. The first is simply to average together the performance scores from a large battery of different tests. In practical IQ measurement, this is the method most commonly used. Perhaps this is one reason why many people have a natural preference for Thomson's model. What could seem more natural than to interpret average success on a wide variety of tasks as the average efficiency of a wide variety of separate mental processes?

However, there is also the second method. This is to use simple visual puzzles like Raven's Matrices—which gives almost the same result. Now, by the standards of experimental psychology, solving Raven's Matrices is a rather complex task. As I have said, we would be hard pressed to say exactly what cognitive processes contribute to it. But does it really seem right to think that it could be a good average measure of all the brain's most important modules? For example, the temporal lobes contain vast stores of facts about the world. When the temporal lobes degenerate, producing a condition called "semantic dementia," the person gradually loses most of this knowledge, until he or she no longer knows a tiger from a fish or a chair from a table.[2] Or to take another example—I already spoke about amnesia, or loss of ability to form new memories. This also depends on the temporal lobes, though not the same part. Or think of all the subtleties of language. Or auditory perception. As I said before, scientists are good at making stories, and doubtless we could imagine how all of these separate processes and functions contribute to Raven's Matrices. The argument, however, is beginning to seem quite stretched.

If the Thomson idea seems wrong here, then we are back to Spearman and to the idea that Raven's Matrices measure something relatively specific—perhaps some particular brain property or process. Given modern ideas of mind and brain, what might this something be? What is there in the brain that could plausibly look like g—something that is always involved when we build an effective, well-structured, "intelligent" piece of behavior?

In 1980 I had just begun work for Britain's Medical Research Council. One of the first projects I was given concerned driving accidents and how they might be avoided. With another postdoctoral scientist, Frank McKenna, I spent part of each week at a London Transport training school, giving psychological tests to trainee bus drivers. We hoped to identify who would do well in training and perhaps who would go on to drive most safely. We had to wear white coats, not because we were handling dangerous reagents, but because the London Transport staff felt that white coats might encourage the trainees to take these two apparently pointless people more seriously. (I think everybody was horrified by how young we were.) This worked quite well. Everybody called us "The Professors."

Each trainee was given two hours of tests: one set from me and another set from Frank. There was only one free room in the school itself, so I worked indoors while Frank ran his tests on the upper floor of a superannuated red London double-decker bus, abandoned outside in a parking lot. Through a long winter, he and his subjects froze together. We ran people in pairs. One person would freeze with Frank for an hour in the bus while a second person stayed inside with me; then for the second hour, the person who had completed Frank's tests would come inside to warm up with me, while the person I had tested would go outside to cool down with Frank. From the trainees' perspective, these were two free hours away from lectures on bus engines. A few paper-and-pencil tests with the young professors were fine with them.

Early on I came across a problem. One of the tests I was using concerned focusing and switching attention. (We thought that the ability to focus and switch might be related to good driving—indeed, some previous work by a group in Israel seemed to suggest this.[3] Our test was copied from theirs.) In this test (this will sound familiar from chapter 1), the person heard two rapid series of words, one presented through headphones to the left ear and the other to the right. The two series ran simultaneously and in synchrony. Each series had a few numbers mixed in among the other words. The subject was supposed to listen to one series and, whenever he heard a number, to repeat it out loud.

Each run lasted just a few seconds. At the start, the subject received an instruction telling him which ear to listen to. The instruction was a tone played over the headphones. A high tone meant listen to the right ear, while a low tone meant listen to the left. Near the end of the run, the two series of words were interrupted by a second tone, again high or low. This tone told the subject which side to listen to for the remainder of the run—again, high right, low left. So, if the second tone was the same as the first one, the subject kept listening to the same side as before; but if it was the other tone, he had to switch ears. By monitoring which numbers he reported, we could tell which side he was listening to at any given moment. We wanted to measure how well he could focus attention for a while on one side, then if necessary switch to the other.

This was the problem. The task began with some instructions from me, then a practice run. Then I would ask the subject to explain the rules back to me, and if he was correct, we would go on with the test. Soon, I began to notice people who did something curious. They understood the instructions perfectly. They could tell me exactly what they should do. Then, when the test began, a part was missing. Although the second tone sounded on each trial and was certainly audible, the subject seemed oblivious. Clearly he did not switch ears, but more than this, he did not hesitate or seem uncertain. Whatever tone he heard, he continued confidently with what he was already doing, just as though nothing had happened. In the subject's description of the rules, this part of the task was present. In performance, it seemed not to exist.

Obviously, I could not use the data from these subjects; to all appearances, they had not even tried to switch their attention. About one subject in every five or six, I found myself throwing the data away. Soon, I thought that the problem might be avoided if I did things differently. My new idea was to ignore what subjects told me about the rules. Instead, I made them continue with practice, pointing out whenever they went wrong, until they had proved that they would stay on the same side when the tone told them to stay and switch when the tone told them to switch. This meant a lot of practice for some subjects, maybe as many as twelve practice runs before we started the main test. Finally, though, the reminders always worked. The subject lost his apparent satisfaction with what he was doing, began to hesitate when the tones sounded, and soon afterward, the lost part of the task would appear.

However, another problem now surfaced. Both Frank's session and mine were a full hour, and as soon as two people were finished, two more would be waiting. If one pair ran late, the next pair would start behind, and on a bad morning, we would be sending the last people back to class half an hour or more after they were supposed to have finished. If my person needed a good number of practice trials in the selective attention test, he or she was almost certain to go over the hour. If my person came late from their first hour with Frank and then needed a lot of practice trials with me, we would end up especially late.

One morning this was happening—my subject had arrived late

from the frozen wastes outside, and now he was having trouble in the selective attention test—it was maybe 1:15 p.m., and we weren't even close to our lunch. As I continued with the practice trials, I was thinking, "Why does this *always* seem to happen that a person who is late from Frank also has problems with me?" I wanted to eat.

Then from nowhere my mind began to make connections. The sudden thrill of a moment like this is hard to describe; I was immediately beside myself with excitement; my heart began to pound. Faster than I can write it down, the world shifted to a new shape. The speed and exhilaration of such a moment is very beautifully described in one chapter of Primo Levi's *The Periodic Table*.

I thought: Actually I know why this happens. Frank's people are late when they do badly on the Embedded Figures Test. That's the one that can really take time if people find it difficult. So the people who do badly on Embedded Figures must be the same people who don't follow my instructions.

I thought: What's the real problem for the people who don't follow instructions? I repeat the same rules over and over, trying to force behavior into shape. The subjects, meanwhile, seem somehow *passive*. They have the information that they need to direct their behavior. They hear the tones; they know the rules; they can actually do the task. But if I don't force them to put all this together, somehow things just don't happen. These subjects don't *zero in* on the part that they know is missing, the exact something to put right. They don't grab the task, pinpoint what it needs, and shake it into shape.

I thought: And it's the same thing in Embedded Figures. In this test, the subject is shown a simple target shape. Then there is a complex, colored design with shapes that are part of other shapes that are part of other shapes, and the subject must find the simple target camouflaged somewhere inside. A look at figure 4 shows the principle. I had been puzzling for months over how people could sometimes find this

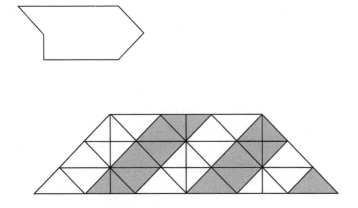

Figure 4. Embedded Figures Test. You must find the shape
shown at the top hidden in the picture at the bottom.

so difficult. Some shapes were certainly hard to find, buried among
all the others, but even so, how could people look for *three minutes* at
one of these pictures and still not find the answer? (Three minutes
was the maximum time allowed for each problem, with twelve problems in total. Some people found hardly any of their targets, so they
would be staring for three minutes at each one. Now you can imagine why this was the test that could make Frank's whole session run
late.)

Suddenly I knew what was going on—or, more exactly, what was
not going on—in a subject's mind during those three minutes. Having been tested by Frank myself, I knew that, in these problems, it
is no use simply waiting for the target shape to appear. Instead you
must take control, just as you will have done yourself with figure 4.
You must take the simple shape and break it into parts. (In figure 4,
you might take the angle at the right-hand end.) Then with this part
fixed in your mind, you go into the complex picture looking just
for that. (In figure 4, you might find an angle of this sort in several

places.) Once this part has been found, you switch to a new line of attack: Can the adjacent lines also be found? Can the whole shape be grown? It is like *giving yourself instructions.*

To me it made no sense to believe that someone who broke the problem up in this way, actively reorganizing and refocusing, could continue for three minutes without success. That meant that only one conclusion was possible: Failure had to mean that the whole pattern of active control, active reorganization, and active division of the problem into parts was missing. Now it made sense that it *would* be the same people who had difficulty with both Frank's test and mine. Both tests were measuring the same thing: the ability to take active charge of a piece of behavior, focus on the part that needed attention, and *make it happen.*

And suddenly this sounded very familiar. In neuropsychology there was a type of patient who had trouble with active shaping of what they did. These were people with damage to the frontal lobes of the brain. I had read a bit of Luria (I will have much more to say about him), and I knew his picture of the frontal lobe patient as inert, driven by the environment, unable to plan, organize, take control.[4] I had also been listening to Tim Shallice, a colleague at the Medical Research Council who was currently developing Luria's ideas. In fact, I knew that frontal lobe patients sometimes did *exactly what my subjects were doing.* They might know what *ought* to be done but somehow not do it, as if knowledge and performance were disconnected. In the case of the patient, this could be even more bizarre. He might say that he should stop doing something—for example, "I know you don't want me to cut the string" or "I know this is wrong"—while at the exact same moment he continued to do it.[5] My people were milder, but they were doing the same thing. They said, "I know the low tone means listen to the left," and sometimes between runs they said, "I know I'm doing it wrong," but when the tones were played, there was no hint of this knowledge in what these subjects actually did. I thought: Both Frank's test and mine are actually measuring frontal lobe function.

The Embedded Figures Test was supposed to measure something called a "field dependent cognitive style." However, we had already realized that, to a large extent, this was actually just another good measure of g. At the time I didn't know that much about g—I certainly hadn't read Spearman—but I did know enough to realize that it was the big one in the study of cognitive abilities, and I had included a standard test of g (Cattell's main test of fluid intelligence, very similar to Raven's Matrices) in the set of tests we were giving to our bus drivers. So the people who did badly on Frank's test were also doing badly on my standard g test. So g itself was really a measure of frontal lobe function. I was looking at a neurophysiological explanation for one of the central discoveries in psychology.

I can't really be certain how much of this was already clear in my mind by the time I raced into lunch to tell Frank about it. Very possibly all of it, and more—certainly I had a whole list of further ideas about why this would matter for driving (all those turned out to be wrong; in fact, g is barely related at all to driving accidents). I do know that my heart was still pounding (an unusual reaction to the London Transport drivers' canteen) and that I didn't really know what I ate (fortunately, no doubt). Frank thought I was getting a bit carried away.

It was a long time before I had a chance to turn any of these ideas into experiments. However, I did begin to devour everything I could find about the frontal lobes. For a while it was like falling in love (in fact, I can still get this back with a bit of thought), and it isn't straightforward turning love into science. The first time I tried to put my ideas onto paper, they were like a love letter. You should probably never show a love letter to anybody except the person it is addressed to, and I'm still grateful to the senior colleague who told me kindly that the ideas "needed more work." View them as objectively as you will, however, the frontal lobes still turn out to be fascinating.

A look back at figure 3 in chapter 3 shows that the frontal lobes make up a substantial part of the human cerebral cortex. They are also relatively large in our closest relatives (apes and monkeys), and in the analysis of frontal lobe functions, experiments with humans and monkeys have gone hand in hand.

A different brain view is shown in figure 5. Remember that the brain has two cerebral hemispheres, left and right. In figure 5, the right hemisphere has been left intact, but the tip of the left hemisphere has been sliced off to show the structure of the frontal lobe more clearly. From this perspective it can be seen that each frontal lobe is like a three-sided pyramid, coming to a point at the front. One of the three surfaces is across the bottom. As it rests above the orbit of the eye, this one is called the orbital surface. Second is the vertical surface in the middle of the brain, where each frontal lobe butts up against the other. This is called the medial surface (in anatomy, "medial" means middle). Third is the outside surface (as previously shown in figure 3), curving around from the top of the medial surface to the outer edge of the orbital surface. This one is called lateral.

As I described in chapter 3, the very back of the lateral surface is the motor cortex—cortex directly concerned with commands for movement. Immediately anterior to (forward from) this is the "premotor cortex," concerned with higher-order aspects of movement such as commands to reach out and pick something up. In the monkey, a further small step forward from the premotor cortex takes you into the "frontal eye field." Neurons here discharge when the monkey makes a voluntary eye movement, and direct electrical stimulation of this part of the brain makes the eye move. In a similar position, the human brain also has something very like a frontal

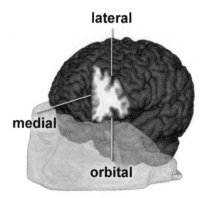

Figure 5. A view of the brain with
the tip of the left hemisphere sliced
off to show the three surfaces of the
frontal lobe.

eye field. At the top and back of the medial surface are several more
motor-related areas.

Even all together, though, these motor regions take up only a
small part of the frontal lobe, toward the back. This leaves us with an
enormous, anterior part whose functions are much more mysterious.
When I say "the frontal lobes" in this book, it is really all this part,
anterior to movement areas, that I mean. Patients with damage to
this large, anterior part of the frontal lobes can have things seriously
wrong with them. They will sometimes have great trouble returning
to their former lives—to their families, their jobs, their friends. But
what is it that has gone wrong? It is nothing simple like loss of sight
or language or memory. It is actually hard to say exactly what it is,
though you may recognize it when you see it. Very often, apparent
steps forward in understanding the frontal lobes have the peculiar
result of leaving you exactly back where you started. I once heard the
frontal lobe called "the graveyard of the neuropsychologist."

❖

There is a feature of our lives that is so universal we are quite un-aware of it. Consider anything that you do—getting up in the morning, preparing a meal, sitting down to read this book. Any of these activities is in fact a complex, organized structure of component thoughts and actions. To organize yourself in a room with my book, you had to find time in the day to read . . . remember where the book had been left . . . navigate a complex environment to that place . . . direct your eyes to show exactly where and how the book lay . . . control movements of arm and hand to pick it up . . . probably find a chair and make all those adjustments it takes to move a human body into a comfortable sitting position . . . remember how far you had read and now open the book to that page . . . bring back into mind what the current section discusses. All these steps are necessary before you can even begin the actual process of reading and thinking, the process that gives this whole sequence its purpose or point. It is the same with the cows I once watched in the river and with each separate person on the square in Havana. The plan of the cow that leaves the river to eat may be simpler than the plan of the fishermen who steer their boat toward the harbor, but in both cases, an extended structure of action—an elaborate mental program—moves the animal or person step by step to the goal.

Evidently, something in the brain must generate these complex structures of goal-directed action. To pose the problem in a little more detail: Through an animal's lifetime, the brain builds up enormous stores of knowledge. Essentially this knowledge describes how the world is and how it works—that there is grass at the top of the river-bank, that the sea contains fish and that nets will catch them, that traffic must progress in only one direction along the street beside the hotel, that people are watching and will judge how the children are dressed. As behavior is constructed, this knowledge must be used to select and assemble just the right steps—the right mental program to move us from where we are to where we wish to be.

Probably our most sophisticated thinking on frontal lobe functions comes from a Russian neuropsychologist, Aleksandr Romanovich Luria. Luria spent a lifetime in clinical and scientific work, describing and analyzing many neuropsychological conditions. He popularized Mr. S, a man with phenomenal memory linked to highly unusual sensory imagery. He worked on varieties of aphasia, or language impairment; apraxia, or movement impairment; and disturbances of visual perception and attention. Much of his early material came from the study of gunshot wounds to the head in World War II. As an active clinician, however, Luria dealt with a daily fare of patients suffering strokes, brain tumors, head injuries, and other kinds of brain disease. The frontal lobes were among his particular fascinations.

Luria proposed that the frontal lobes are essential for constructing organized behavioral sequences. In the patient with frontal lobe damage, accordingly, the goal-directed structure of activity is broken. Instead of leading clearly from A to B, behavior sequences can be interrupted by things that at best don't belong, at worst are actively obstructive. Alternatively, some obvious and essential part of the sequence—something that has to be included if the goal is to be achieved—may be left out. In itself, the sequence that is impaired can be anything—looking at a picture to discover its meaning, retelling a story, copying an experimenter's actions, solving a puzzle. This is what makes the frontal lobe patient's difficulty so hard to define. It is not the detail of the particular behavior that matters—as it is, for example, for a patient with occipital lobe damage who cannot recognize the objects he or she sees, the patient with left temporal and parietal lobe damage who cannot understand speech, the patient with right parietal damage who ignores the left side of space. For the frontal lobe patient, the individual fragments of thought and behavior may all be preserved. It is the active process of organizing these into a useful, overall structure that has gone wrong.

Of course, Luria was not the only person, or even the first person, to realize something along these lines. In the late nineteenth century, an Italian neuroscientist, Leonardo Bianchi, carried out surgical removals of the frontal lobe in monkeys. After surgery, he found that his animals retained all the basic components of their behavior. They could see and hear, look around themselves, move normally, feed. As Bianchi put it, however, their behavior as a whole had lost its purposeful structure. Here is an example:

> The monkey which used to jump on to the window-ledge, to call out to his companions, after the operation jumps on to the ledge again, but does not call out. The sight of the window determines the reflex of the jump, but the purpose is now lacking, for it is no longer represented in the focal point of consciousness. . . . Another monkey sees the handle of the door and grasps it, but the mental process stops at the sight of the bright colour of the handle; the animal does not attempt to turn it so as to open the door, but sits on it. Evidently there are lacking all those other images that are necessary for the determination of a series of movements co-ordinated towards one end.[6]

Another striking example comes from an American neurosurgeon, Wilder Penfield, working in the early 1930s. At around age forty, Penfield's sister was diagnosed with an infiltrating tumor affecting the right frontal lobe. Penfield himself performed surgery to remove it, and in 1935 he published a description of the results.[7] His account once more points up the strange riddles of frontal lobe function.

On the one hand are the things that are preserved—even during an enormous frontal lobe removal. In the case of Penfield's sister, surgery was performed under local anesthesia, and through the long hours it took, the patient kept up a running conversation about her children, at the end apologizing "for having made so much trouble."

After recovery, she lived for awhile longer before finally dying of brain hemorrhage into the recurring tumor. During this time "her sense of humour, memory, and insight into the thought and feelings of others was altogether unimpaired. She was capable of intelligent conversation and did not talk either more or less than good taste demanded." Her letters showed "insight, vivid memory and power of expression."[8]

But, there were also profound changes. Here is Penfield's most famous example:

> One day about fifteen months after [the] operation she had planned to get a simple supper for one guest (W.P.) and four members of her own family. She looked forward to it with pleasure and had the whole day for preparation. This was a thing she could have done with ease ten years before. When the appointed hour arrived she was in the kitchen, the food was all there, one or two things were on the stove, but the salad was not ready, the meat had not been started and she was distressed and confused by her long continued effort alone. It seemed evident that she would never be able to get everything ready at once. With help the task of preparation was quickly completed and the occasion went off successfully with the patient talking and laughing in an altogether normal way.[9]

According to Penfield, the defect produced was "a lack of capacity for planned administration." His sister put it more simply. She "could not think well enough," was a little "slow," a little "incapable." Once again, profound deficits, not in the fragments of behavior, but in how they are put together to move from A (problem started) to B (problem solved).

The best way to get a flavor of Luria's thinking is to look at some examples. You do have to be careful with Luria. He was working, of course, long before the days of brain scans, so that his information about precise areas of brain damage would often have been poor. His writing, furthermore, tends to be more impressionistic than we expect from a modern Western scientist. Often, it is hard to be sure exactly which behavior was shown by exactly which patient; Luria is more concerned to give an overall impression of what "the typical" frontal lobe patient is like. To get across his point, he also tended to emphasize extreme patients—certainly more extreme than the typical patient with a frontal lobe stroke or tumor. In many cases, in fact, patients with small areas of frontal lobe damage can look remarkably normal after a few months of recovery. Just the same, I think most neuropsychologists would agree that, though perhaps almost a caricature, Luria's essential picture is right. The examples here all come from his book *Higher Cortical Functions in Man.*

At its most extreme, the world of Luria's patients was behavioral chaos. He describes a patient who, planing a plank in the hospital carpenter's shop, continued right through to the bottom and then began planing the bench. Certainly a patient of this sort is capable of discriminating between plank and bench; somehow, the information just gets lost as the behavior unfolds. Another patient might be attracted by the sight of the call button by the bed, press it, but then have no request for the nurse who answered. A patient might ignore the doctor questioning him by the bedside but instead answer questions directed to the person in the next bed. When things can go this wrong, more than ever it brings into focus how much we are all doing all of the time to make things go right. So many wrong turns avoided at every moment of the day. Something in the brain—something powerful and complex—has to be there to make this happen.

The patient's behavior can be derailed at any phase of a task. One of the deficits Luria emphasized was in "preliminary investigative activity." When we face a new problem, there is typically a phase of examining its relevant conditions and properties—actively probing to see what matters in this corner of the world, what needs to be done, and what methods are available to do it. One of Luria's favorite problems, for example, was called Link's cube. The subject is given twenty-seven small cubes. Some of them have three yellow faces and three blue faces. Some have two yellow and four blue, others one yellow and five blue. One is all blue. Using these components, the subject is told to construct a single large cube whose outer surface is entirely yellow. The normal person begins by picking up the cubes, examining them, working out what sort of cubes are available, and forming a plan of attack. Then he proceeds to assemble his solution. Instead, the frontal lobe patient immediately begins piling cubes together. He has no idea of what materials he is working with or where his actions will take him. With the preliminary investigation left out, he has no chance of success.

Equally, Luria emphasized a failure to compare the results of action with the intended goal. Asked to determine the situation depicted in a painting or to solve an arithmetical problem, patients would seize on some salient feature of the materials—a particular person in the foreground of the picture or a particular pair of numbers that might be added together—generate a confident solution based just on these fragments, and offer it in complete disregard of strong clues that this solution could not possibly be correct. Or asked to retell a fairy story, the patient might begin to incorporate material from his own life—perhaps an account of how he had once been a barber in a small town—apparently unconcerned by its obvious irrelevance to the task at hand.

Another of Luria's favorite concepts was "inertia"—passively following some behavioral path of least resistance instead of actively ensuring that tasks stayed on track. Patients might be dominated by strong or familiar responses to things in the environment. For example, a patient asked to raise her hand when the experimenter tapped a pencil might instead tap the hand, mimicking the environment instead of correctly following the instruction. Patients were also dominated by a tendency to "perseverate"—to repeat a previous, now unwanted action. For example, the patient is asked to draw two circles and a minus sign. The circles are drawn correctly, but perseverating the tendency to draw large, open figures, the minus sign is then drawn as a horizontal rectangle. The patient is now asked to draw another circle. He draws the circle, adds inside this the horizontal rectangle that was previously produced, then writes at the bottom, "No entry." Another behavioral structure distorted by intrusion of bizarre, irrelevant fragments.

I have already described one way in which frontal lobe patients can resemble low-g subjects in the London Transport study. Occasionally, they show a striking mismatch between what they *know* of a task's requirements and what they actually *do*. Here is one of Luria's examples. The patient is asked to squeeze a rubber bulb when a light is switched on. When the light appears, the patient says, "I must squeeze!"—and does nothing. To get the correct behavior out of the patient, the experimenter must repeat "Squeeze!" every time the light comes on—just as, at London Transport, enough prompting from me would always finally bring out the missing response to tones.

In fact, just like my difficulties at London Transport, Luria describes particular difficulties for the frontal lobe patient in following instructions—in translating what he or she has been told into "new systems of motor acts." Here is his account of the frontal lobe patient back at work: "The supervisor's instructions could not be converted into a true motive for activity"—the necessary plan being replaced by a "single, inertly reproduced operation or by a series of impulsive fragments."[10]

When I discovered *Higher Cortical Functions in Man*, I also found that Luria had been there well before me as regards the Embedded Figures Test. Here is his account of frontal lobe patients attempting a very similar search for a target shape camouflaged within a larger pattern: "unable to actively pick out the required part of the pattern from the whole, even if first shown to him . . . Patients with frontal lobe lesions showed considerable difficulty in all such tests, readily slipping back to the 'strong' structure."[11]

In much of this, there is an unsettling sense that the frontal lobe patient is very much like the rest of us—but more so. Perhaps we all have the experience of wondering *how* we could have missed something so obvious in a problem we tried to solve or an action we failed to complete. We "knew" what should be done, but somehow, just at that moment, the knowledge failed to surface. To some extent, the frontal lobe patient seems like a caricature of ourselves—muddled, imperfect, confused.

Here is Luria's own summary of what this all amounts to: "The plan of . . . actions, involving the patient's intentions, quickly loses its regulating influence on behaviour as a whole and is replaced by per-severations of one particular link of the motor act or by the influence of some connection established during the patient's past experience. This form of disturbance of the system of selective, goal-directed actions, with their replacement by inert motor stereotypes or frag-mentary irrelevant connections, may be detected in many patients with a frontal lobe lesion."[12]

At first sight, it seems that frontal lobe functions, as described by Luria, would have to be a key part of g. By definition, g reflects those aspects of cognitive function that affect all manner of different activities. Of necessity, any such function will be reflected in positive manifold and be measured as part of g. As I have argued, *anything* we do involves a complex, coordinated structure of thought and action. For any task, this structure can be better or worse—the structure is optimized as we settle into the task, searching for good strategies, realizing what is important, "keeping our eye on the ball." One of the great pleasures of life is to do something new and to work out how to do it well. According to Luria's ideas, the frontal lobes are essential in this process. If they do their job well, mental programs in general should be well constructed. If they work less well, this should be reflected in poorer or less optimal programs. Because everything in biology varies, it seems certain that frontal lobe functions will be stronger in some people than others. If this has a general effect on whatever people undertake, it must surely be reflected in g.

Furthermore, an enormous research literature on frontal lobe patients does show deficits in every conceivable variety of cognitive test. These include tests of perception, learning mazes, memory for lists of words, responding as fast as possible to simple lights or shapes, copying gestures, using real-world knowledge such as how to plan a holiday or order a meal in a restaurant, naming as many words as possible that begin with the letter F, and many more. In neuropsychology, some tests have become popular to "assess" frontal lobe function, but in my opinion, it is almost a matter of chance which tests these are. As I have said, most frontal lobe patients do not show the extreme collapse in behavior that Luria describes. Still, if we compare a reasonably large group of frontal lobe patients with a similar group of undamaged control subjects, my belief is that most tasks will show a deficit in the patients. Just as Luria's ideas imply, frontal lobe patients show an across-the-board loss in effective action—as they should if g has been reduced.

On all of these grounds, it seems obvious to conclude that frontal lobe functions must be a major part of g. It is also obvious that the deficits of frontal lobe patients are closely linked to our everyday ideas of "intelligence." Perhaps most cultures have a group that they pick on with "stupid person" jokes: The English tell jokes about the

Irish, Americans tell jokes about the Poles, the Dutch tell jokes about the Belgians, Argentinians tell jokes about Spaniards, people from Tokyo tell jokes about people from Osaka. But these jokes could just as easily be jokes about frontal lobe patients. Here are two (though I have never discovered who tells such jokes about the English, perhaps because they are too busy mocking our food and diffidence, here I shall give it a try):

> Charles thinks the turn-signal may not be working on his car. He asks Hugo to help him test it. After a bit of thought, they come up with a plan. Charles says, "I'll get in the car and press the switch. You stand at the back and tell me whether the light comes on." Charles gets into the car, and Hugo goes to the back. Charles presses the switch. He yells, "Is it working?" Hugo says, "Yes it is . . . no it's not . . . yes it is . . . no it's not . . . ."

> A Limey has just crossed over to America from Liverpool. He's delighted with his new home in the land of the free, and to celebrate becoming an American, he decides to go to his first baseball game. He buys a burger and a Coke, heads down to the front of the stands, and settles in with satisfaction to watch the game.
>
> He's just taking the first bite into his burger when he hears from somewhere high up in the stands a man calling out, "Hey . . . Pete!" He stands up, looks around, but can't see anybody he knows. So he sits down again, but just as he's getting ready to take another bite, again he hears the voice: "Hey . . . Pete!" Slightly aggravated, he gets up to look around again, but again he can't see anybody he knows. (Why would he? He just arrived on the boat.) He shrugs, sits down again, is just about to pick up the burger, when for the third time he hears: "Hey . . . Pete!" Now thoroughly annoyed he jumps back to his feet. He turns around and yells, "My name's not Pete!"

Don't these both sound exactly like Luria's description of the frontal lobe patient? In both cases, there is some obvious information that we know the person must have. Everybody knows that indicators flash. Everybody knows that the name you shout indicates who you are shouting at. But in the stupid person joke, this obvious information somehow gets left out of consideration. There is a structure of thought or behavior with a large chunk missing . . . just as there is in Luria's frontal failures.

This line of thought brings us to a paradox. When I first began to read the frontal lobe literature, almost everybody agreed on one point. Frontal lobe patients were disorganized, used poor strategies, got distracted. Most of what they did, they often did badly. But this had nothing to do with conventional "intelligence." If you believed the literature of that time, about the only thing a frontal lobe patient reliably performed well on was a standard IQ test. In light of Spearman's theory and definition of g, what sense could this possibly make?

Many of the reasons for the conventional belief went back to early studies in the 1940s and 1950s. In fact, when you looked at these reasons, they weren't especially strong—though they do show the power of an authoritative voice in science. One of the most influential thinkers in twentieth-century work on the brain, Donald Hebb, carried out an early study with Wilder Penfield, the man whose sister I described earlier. The subject was a single young man who, following a major frontal lobe injury, was left with epilepsy and severe personality problems. In the hope of improving things, a large part of both frontal lobes was removed, and after surgery, the patient's IQ was not too bad. Most people, indeed, thought his behavior was generally improved despite the large amount of his brain that had been removed. In fact, his IQ had not been measured before his original injury, and Hebb and Penfield themselves were clear that they did not really know if frontal lobe damage had changed it. Nevertheless, this paper is still cited to show that the frontal lobes have little to do with IQ.[13]

Another landmark was the work of Hans-Lukas Teuber, deservedly a godfather of American neuropsychology. After World War II, Teuber and his associates set up a major study of long-term consequences of missile wounds in the head. The program was unique, incorporating more than a hundred ex-soldiers, each of whose injuries was delineated as carefully as possible using entrance wounds, field surgeon's notes, and evidence of shell fragments or other foreign bodies still in the brain. The work produced a large number of important reports contrasting the effects of damage to different brain regions. As one part of this program, Teuber and his colleague Sidney Weinstein analyzed IQ scores for more than fifty of their patients.[14] They found no deficit specifically linked to frontal lobe damage. Teuber concluded that "ordinary intelligence tests are especially unsuitable" for showing the effects of frontal lobe damage.[15] Over the next decades, the weight of Teuber's opinion came to dominate neuropsychological thinking.

In retrospect, I wonder now whether war wounds provide a poor way to study frontal lobe damage. Luria, for example, often admits that the major problems he describes are most clearly seen in people with a great deal of damaged brain—for example, people with large, rapidly growing tumors invading a good proportion of both frontal lobes. In contrast, as I mentioned previously, impairments are often modest when the extent of frontal damage is small. Of course, Weinstein and Teuber did not have brain scans to assess the question, but it does seem likely that something like a shell fragment may often leave quite a minor region of damage. In fact, in Teuber's whole research program, which involved many kinds of cognitive function, strong, consistent deficits linked to frontal lobe damage seemed few and far between—a strikingly different picture from Luria's.

Even if I am wrong about this, there is a second issue with the Weinstein and Teuber study. The IQ test they used was called the Army General Classification Test. They used the test because it allowed them to compare IQs before and after injury; all their patients were ex-soldiers, so the army had given them this test when they entered the service. (By this time, Spearman's speculation about using a test of Greek syntax to select men to command troops had turned into reality—with a few modifications.) This is predominantly a verbal test. In line with this, Weinstein and Teuber found the worst performance in patients with lesions of the left temporal and parietal lobes—exactly the kind that should be most harmful for language.

Such findings immediately recall the concepts of crystallized and fluid intelligence from chapter 2. The crystallized test measures knowledge—verbal tests in particular are like this—whereas the fluid test measures current ability to solve novel problems. As we saw, these different tests can agree in the normal population—both giving a more or less similar measure of g—but they can behave very differently when the brain is changed. Might it be that a fluid intelligence test—something more like Raven's Matrices—would show results very different from Weinstein and Teuber's?

In the early 1990s I had my first chance to test this idea. I have mentioned Hebb and Penfield and Weinstein and Teuber, but their work is not alone. The literature is studded with occasional frontal lobe patients whose cognitive deficits are obvious and substantial—for example, patients who have become disorganized, sometimes unemployable in everyday life—but whose IQs are still very high. Of course, these people are not easy to find. People with high IQs are rare in themselves; people with frontal lobe damage are rare; and people who have frontal lobe damage, whose IQ was very high and remains so, who come to the attention of a research neuropsychologist, and who are willing to help in an experiment are gold dust. Around 1992, however, a colleague, Paul Burgess, identified three of these people from among hundreds of patients he had worked with. All three were remarkable for their substantial damage to the frontal lobes, obvious cognitive impairments, yet IQs above 125. (In conventional IQ testing, the average person in the population gets a score of 100. The details of how this is done are not important—an arbitrary scheme for translating performance into numbers simply guarantees that the average score will be 100. Only around 5 percent of people get a score of 125 or more.) We decided to look at these high IQs again with a different test.[16]

Remember that there are two ways to obtain a measure of g. The first is simply to average together performance on a large battery of different subtests. It does not matter much what these are, just that they should be diverse. This is by far the most common approach in clinical neuropsychology. In particular it is the approach in the Wechsler Adult Intelligence Scale, or WAIS—the test that had previously been given to our three patients.

Of course, individual subtests in the WAIS need not have especially high g saturations on their own. (Remember from chapter 2 that the g saturation of a test reflects the relative contributions of g and s; the higher the g saturation, the better is the test for measuring g.) Some subtests, furthermore, are obviously crystallized rather than fluid. They assess knowledge such as vocabulary, not current ability to solve new problems.

The second method is to use a test that, all on its own, has the highest possible g saturation. These are the fluid intelligence tests such as Raven's Matrices. The test we actually used is called Cattell's Culture Fair—the same test I had used at London Transport. We called back each of the three patients and gave them this fluid intelligence test.

The first person we tested was an ex-businessman. After his stroke, he had been forced to retire. He had become distractible, inefficient, unable to deliver. None of these problems was reflected in his WAIS IQ, which was 126. When we gave him the Culture Fair, it produced an IQ 38 points lower at 88. Quite possibly it was not the whole story, but one major thing that had happened to this person was an enormous loss in fluid intelligence.

The other two people were similar, though less extreme. (It is a peculiar quirk of life in experimental psychology that the first results always seem to be the best.) The second was an ex-schoolteacher with a WAIS IQ of 130. He had lost much of one frontal lobe when a large object was driven into his head in a car accident. The Culture Fair gave an IQ of 108. For the third person, the WAIS IQ was 126, the Culture Fair IQ 97.

Nobody liked the results of this experiment. When work is submitted for publication in a scientific journal, the editor invites critical reviews from two or three other scientists in the field. The reviewers assess the work and give an opinion on whether it should be published. Our paper received the most waspish reviews that I have ever seen: I keep them to cheer up younger colleagues when they get reviews of their own. However, the results finally did appear, and they do help to clear up the paradox of the frontal lobe literature. The senseless idea that frontal lobe patients have normal g but globally impaired behavior evaporates if g is measured properly—with a test of current function, not of lifetime learning.

How could neuropsychology have held onto this peculiar idea for so long? The problem goes back to the two separate roots of "intelligence testing": the practical approach of Binet and the theoretical approach of Spearman. It is the practical approach—the approach in such tests as the WAIS—that has generally dominated in neuropsychology. For a neuropsychologist, the WAIS IQ is just a feature of the landscape, important context in interpreting a patient's other deficits but not something of interest in itself. The picture is very different if you are thinking in terms of Spearman. Now g is a theoretical construct, a proposal about something in the mind. Now a neuropsychologist might well want to know what that something is. In this tradition, one would never use a test like the WAIS. Instead one is led inevitably to fluid intelligence—and to obvious deficits in frontal lobe patients.

On theoretical grounds, we said that a process affecting all manner of behavior must necessarily be linked to g. Now we see that this is confirmed for the behavioral control functions of the frontal lobe. When frontal lesions produce disorganized behavior, this disorganization is reflected in a major loss in g.

Obviously, this simple conclusion can be only a rough approximation. The frontal lobes are very large. Anatomically they are quite heterogeneous, with each part of the frontal lobe having its own, distinct pattern of connections to other structures in the brain. (On arrival in the frontal lobe, however, different kinds of information are rapidly passed around from one part to another.) I will say something later about attempts to divide and conquer within the frontal lobe—to assign different functions to different frontal regions. These attempts have their intriguing successes and failures. Still, if g is related to frontal lobe function, it does seem likely that some parts of the frontal lobe will be more important than others.

In fact, I would now put my original hypothesis a little differently. The evidence we now have suggests a specific set of frontal lobe regions that are most closely connected to g. This new evidence also throws up another cortical area—a region back in the parietal lobes—that is also involved. The new evidence comes from functional brain imaging. This is the method I described in chapter 3 for showing which areas do what as the normal brain works.

In a functional brain imaging study, the experimenter defines some cognitive process of interest. This could be anything: visual object recognition, retrieval from memory, response to emotional pictures, anything. We can call it X. The experimenter designs two tasks, one involving more of X, the other less, but otherwise matched as carefully as possible. The difference in brain activity between these two tasks shows which areas X recruits or calls up.

Modern brain imaging experiments began in the late 1980s with a technique called positron emission tomography, or PET. The basic method for isolating X was developed by Michael Posner, Marcus Raichle, and their group at Washington University in Saint Louis; today hundreds of laboratories worldwide are doing this same thing with MRI machines (functional MRI). In the early 1990s, however, few places could run PET experiments. They are very expensive; they involve inhalation or injection of radioactive oxygen, and because this has a short half-life, the experiments need a cyclotron on-site to produce it. So, though everybody was rushing to report experiments with this new technology, the actual information appeared quite slowly. The early experiments were not very sensitive, either—so when you looked at X, you knew you would see just a part of the brain circuit involved, like the tip of the iceberg. In any one experiment, a lot of brain activity would certainly be missed.

In the early experiments, there were often some areas of activity in the frontal lobes. As these began to appear, experimenters would obviously interpret them in terms of the specific task they had designed: the particular X they were looking at. For example, if it was a language experiment, frontal activity would be explained in terms of language processes; if it was a memory experiment, frontal activity would be explained in terms of memory processes; and so on. At first, PET experiments seemed to be revealing many new modules in the frontal lobes with much more specific functions than anybody had ever supposed— almost a new module for every cognitive function examined, in fact.

As the picture built up, however, something began to look wrong. From one experiment to another, this frontal lobe activity often looked much the same. Though one experiment concerned language, another memory, yet another the effects of practice, still the general pattern of frontal activity was similar. This was especially true considering that any one experiment gave only a partial view of the true X activity, so that to see the whole iceberg, it was necessary to combine information across several similar experiments.

Toward the end of the 1990s, my colleague Adrian Owen and I decided to look at this question more formally.[17] (Of course, many people were beginning to notice the same pattern in their results; we just decided to put some of this information together.) We looked through the experimental literature to find popular cognitive demands—ones that had been looked at quite a few times—to give us the best chance of finding a complete iceberg. We chose five of the best; they were actually Stroop-like experiments in which the subject had to resist making a strong or familiar response (remember, from chapter 1, naming the colors of words while trying not to read the words themselves), practice experiments, experiments on recognizing objects that were hard to identify, and experiments on two aspects of short-term memory. We searched for all the published experiments we could find looking at these five demands and combined the results.

The results failed to show two things. They did not show activity spread over the whole frontal lobe, as might be expected if the whole thing were homogeneous. But neither did the results show real modules—separate frontal areas doing separate things. Instead, just as we had started to suspect, the results suggested that the *same* frontal areas were apparently involved in all these different cognitive activities. Outside the frontal lobe, furthermore, we found something very similar in a region of the parietal lobe: another band of tissue in both hemispheres that seemed to be active when *any* of our cognitive demands was increased.[18]

The pattern of activity is shown in figure 6a. On the left is a view from the right side of the brain, showing activity on the outer or lateral surface. On the right, the left hemisphere has been cut away to show activity on the inner or medial surface of the right hemisphere. Other views would show a symmetrical, matched pattern of activity in the left hemisphere. As the figure shows, there is one band of activity on the lateral frontal surface, toward the rear of the frontal lobe, though in front of the premotor cortex. Another band is on the medial frontal surface, just above the thick cable of axons (wires) that joins one hemisphere to the other. Then there is the additional region I described across the middle of the parietal lobe. Taken together, these three regions seem to form a brain circuit that comes online for *almost any kind* of demanding cognitive activity. For any given demand, of course, this general circuit will be joined by other brain areas specific for the particular task. For example, if the task is visual object recognition, the general circuit will be joined by activity in visual areas. The general circuit, however, is a constant across demands. We call it the "multiple-demand" circuit.

Though we are already getting used to it, it is worth stopping for a moment to remember how extraordinary it is that we can now see brain activity in such detail. When Luria published *Higher Cortical Functions in Man* in the 1960s, the scientist could not even see where damage had occurred in a living person's brain. That changed with the invention of CT scans. When Posner went to Saint Louis to start the PET experiments, for most of us it seemed like a dream to imagine that we could actually track human brain activity as it happened. Now this is taken for granted.

Of course, multiple-demand activity is exactly what should be seen for brain areas related to *g*. It is also what should be seen for Luria's general process of programming or building up effective structures of behavior, whatever the particular behavior itself may be. Importantly, the new functional imaging results do not suggest this activity in

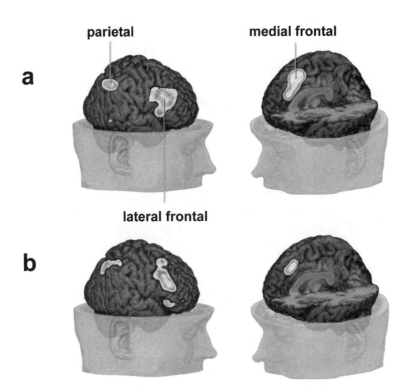

parietal **medial frontal**

a

lateral frontal

b

Figure 6. (a) Pale regions show the multiple-demand circuit—similar regions of brain activity associated with many different tasks. (b) Multiple-demand regions are also linked to g—shown in the pattern of brain activity while solving fluid intelligence problems.

the whole frontal lobe. For example, the third frontal surface—the orbital surface—showed almost nothing in any of the experiments we reviewed. It seems that the multiple-demand regions—not only and not all of the frontal lobes—are most related to g.

Functional brain imaging has also allowed us to look again at the Spearman and Thomson theories. At the start of this chapter, I suggested that correlational data alone could never distinguish the two. Essentially, each theory can mimic the other in the predictions it makes.

The situation might be different, though, with brain data. According to the Spearman theory, g is something specific that contributes to all manner of different tasks. If so, then this something specific might be reflected in a specific pattern of brain activity. This pattern would be seen in many tasks—but it should be especially strong for tasks with high g loadings, tasks such as Raven's Matrices or Cattell's Culture Fair. According to the Thomson theory, on the other hand, these tasks work because they reflect *average* efficiency in many or most of the brain's modules. The special thing about a good task for measuring g is the *breadth* of processes it samples. The best g tasks should sample all the brain's most important modules—reflected in a broad pattern of brain activity across systems involved in language, knowledge, memory, number processing, and so on.

When the experiment is done, it is the Spearman prediction that is confirmed. Specifically, it is the multiple-demand pattern that is seen in high g tasks. In an early PET experiment—carried out with a collaborator, Rüdiger Seitz, at the PET center in Düsseldorf—we used one problem-solving task adapted from the Culture Fair and a second based on letter rather than symbol problems. In each case, we compared the original task with another, modified to take out the problem-solving element and reduce the g correlation. Other experimenters have also compared Raven's Matrices with simpler tasks—and now that we have functional MRI, we can repeat these earlier experiments with even more definite results. Figure 6b shows an example from an experiment in Cambridge for comparison with the multiple-demand pattern in figure 6a. Evidently, the high g task does not show activity all over the cerebral cortex. For example, there is almost nothing in either temporal lobe, the seat of much that is basic to language, memory and knowledge. Instead, figures 6a and 6b are really much the same—with a specific pattern of activity on the lateral and medial frontal surfaces and across the center of the parietal lobes. Again, these multiple-demand regions seem most related to g.[19]

According to Luria, all that we do depends on the behavioral organization functions of the frontal (now also, part of the parietal) lobe. Any activity requires optimal assembly of the right mental program. Just as Spearman thought, this implies a common mental function affecting all kinds of human activities.

In chapter 2, we left for later the question of why complex tasks like Raven's Matrices provide such good measures of g. I suggested that, by their very nature, complex tasks are hard to analyze in terms of underlying psychological processes. If we look back now at the matrix problem in figure 2, however, it really does seem to fit the story of finding and assembling the separate parts of a mental program. To find the correct answer, we must notice and consider the difference in shape between left and right. Then we must notice the difference in size. Then the difference in color from top to bottom. Only if we build a mental program with all of these steps can we know that the fourth choice is correct.[20] Now it seems obvious that this is just the sort of mental programming process—combining separate parts in service of the final goal—that can fail in frontal lobe patients.

In the London Transport study, it was an inconvenience when people described the task's rules but then failed to follow them. We hadn't expected this to happen and certainly hadn't designed the experiment to measure it. Subsequently, though, I have worked on this phenomenon a great deal.[21] Under the right conditions, a good number of people will show this disconnect between what they know and what they do—the same kind of disconnect that Luria describes in frontal lobe patients.

Nowadays we no longer use a tape recorder and tones (they are often inconvenient), but the principle is much the same. For example, there may be two streams of letters and numbers flashing on a computer screen, one to the left and one to the right. For each run, the person begins watching one side, repeating targets (usually letters) out loud. Near the end, a new instruction sometimes tells him to switch sides. This instruction is usually a symbol that flashes in the middle of the screen. Just as we found with the tones, a certain proportion of people complete the whole test in apparent oblivion of these "re-instructions." They don't hesitate or seem concerned that things are going wrong. Somehow, this bit of the task has simply vanished.

Just like Luria's patients, these people always know what they *ought* to do. Even when we ask them again at the end of the whole experiment, subjects always describe the rules correctly. People are also quite *capable* of doing what we ask. We prove this in the same way that I proved it at London Transport. After a series of runs when the instruction is ignored, we begin to prompt people about their failures. After each trial, for example, we might point out what instruction flashed up and what the subject should have done. When this is done, every subject who has previously been failing will soon begin to succeed. We have also tried just asking people at the end of the experiment what happened. Typical responses are that they didn't notice the instruction cues or that they saw them but didn't think about them or that "those went over my head." It really is very like Luria's patients—a sense of passivity, slight cloudiness, a failure of crisp and effective mental focus. A failure to turn instructions into the correct, complete mental program.

Just as we suspected at London Transport, furthermore, this failure is closely related to a conventional test of fluid intelligence. In a typical experiment, about a sixth of the people who are tested will show the phenomenon. These are almost all people with low g scores on a test such as the Culture Fair. A person whose IQ (measured by the

Culture Fair) is below 85 is almost sure to ignore the instruction cues. People with IQs above 100 almost never do. There is only so much that can be taken from this finding. Remembering chapter 2, what we have here is another example of positive manifold. The same people who do badly on the Culture Fair also tend to fail in our tasks—but according to the law of positive manifold, low scores on the Culture Fair always predict difficulties in other tasks. That said, it is not too common to see tasks going from total failure in the lower part of the g distribution to total success in the upper half. This relationship in our tasks does seem important. Just as we thought, the result implies that typical fluid intelligence tests—problem-solving tasks such as Raven's Matrices and the Culture Fair—indeed measure something that is very close to Luria's mental programming. The same people who find these tests difficult also leave gaps in a new mental program, much like the gaps of patients with frontal lobe damage.

There are many uncertain points in this story. Here is an example. As we have seen, multiple-demand activity is strong toward the back of the lateral frontal surface. As tasks become more complex, however, this activity starts to spread forward. For the most difficult problems in Raven's Matrices, for example, activity can extend almost to the tip of the frontal lobes. Are we seeing addition of new mechanisms as tasks become more complex? Or is the posterior part of the system simply the most responsive, so that we see more anterior parts only as demands increase? How much of this activity should be related to g, just the posterior part that is so common for so many different tasks or more anterior parts, too?

Here is another uncertainty. I have already described our first experiments on fluid intelligence after frontal lobe damage, where we focused just on those paradoxical patients with major behavioral impairments but apparently preserved IQs. Since then, we have tested many different kinds of patients (to date almost one hundred) trying to define more exactly what type of damage is important. This is painful, time-consuming work, because the damage that patients have is rarely confined to the particular area of interest. Some people have bigger areas of damage, others much smaller, with exact shapes and sizes varying randomly from one person to the next. Though we have been running this study for more than ten years, we still have only preliminary answers. In the frontal lobe, g is certainly related to the total amount of damage. The bigger the damaged area, the worse the impairment—a point I mentioned earlier in the chapter. This effect of lesion size applies to standard tests of fluid intelligence and to missing task parts in the London Transport tasks; as we should expect, the same patients have problems with both. The importance of lesion size is reassuring: A person really does need to lose quite a lot of the frontal lobe before much is likely to happen. But even after ten years, our results are still incomplete in defining which specific frontal regions are most important. Damage within the multiple-demand regions is more important than damage outside them, but which regions are most important? Are the effects of damage to different multiple-demand regions all the same? Large though this study is, better answers will still require more patients.

There is a similar problem at the back of the brain. Some people with large areas of damage outside the frontal lobes suffer a g decrement. Now that we have seen the multiple-demand results from functional imaging, we know that this should happen. Specifically, it should happen for people with damage in the middle of the parietal lobes. Roughly speaking, this seems to be true, but again, our current answers are quite imprecise. To do better, we need to expend yet more time and effort.

❖

As figure 6 shows, the multiple-demand circuit occupies only a restricted part of the frontal lobe, and certainly there is much more to the frontal lobes than g. One of the most striking features of some frontal lobe patients is a change in social behavior. It is reasonably likely that, with some patients, they will break off in the middle of the testing session to begin unfastening their trousers. Or we can go back to Paul Burgess and the discrepancy between WAIS IQ and fluid intelligence. In one of his tests, Burgess takes patients on a shopping expedition. The patient has a specific set of tasks to carry out, with strict limits on time, money, and which shops to enter. Among other spectacular oddities in this test, one patient found himself clambering over the vegetables on the pavement outside the greengrocer's and, when he ran out of money, proposing his own, rather personal form of payment for a birthday card. Such behavior just cannot be explained by a poor score on Raven's Matrices.

Another friend of mine, Louise Phillips, has made this point rather clearly in the context of aging.[22] Certainly, much of the cognitive change in older people can be explained by a change in g. Old people do worse than young in almost any task they are set—especially fluid intelligence tests. There is also a popular view that cognitive decline in old age reflects changes in frontal lobe function. For example, anatomical changes in the brain can be especially strong in the frontal lobe. The social aspect of frontal lobe damage, however, is just not right for old age. Elderly people may often do badly on fluid intelligence tests, and they may be disorganized in approaching new tasks—but they do not interrupt these tasks to unfasten their trousers. Obviously, some additional change has occurred in many frontal lobe patients, something that is not like the effect of aging and not like a change in g.

This line of thought brings us back to the divide-and-conquer issue. The frontal lobes are large and complex. Plausibly, different parts of the frontal lobes have somewhat different functions. For much of the brain, separating the functions of different regions has worked outstandingly well. For the frontal lobe, the picture is more complicated.

Probably this divide-and-conquer thinking does help us with the problem of disturbed social behavior in some frontal lobe patients. For many years, people have suggested that social and emotional disturbances come from damage to the orbital surface—the surface that is completely left out of the multiple-demand picture—and perhaps the adjacent, lower parts of the medial surface. For example, the most famous frontal lobe patient is Phineas Gage, a railroad construction foreman who, in 1848, had a meter-long metal rod blown through the anterior part of his frontal lobe. Modern reconstructions suggest major damage to the orbital and medial surfaces. The result of this damage was a spectacular set of changes, not in cognition, but in personality. A man who had been responsible, trustworthy, and capable became "fitful, irreverent, indulging at times in the grossest profanity . . . his mind was radically changed, so decidedly that his friends and acquaintances said he was 'no longer Gage.'"[23]

To prove that disturbances like these come from orbital/medial damage, the strongest evidence would be a pattern of results called a "double dissociation." In the ideal pattern, randomly selected patients with orbital/medial damage would show more social than cognitive impairment, whereas randomly selected patients with other frontal damage would show the reverse pattern. Assembling large, random patient groups is not so easy to do, and as in the case of Gage, impressions in this field come largely from isolated (if striking) clinical cases. Still, functional brain imaging does support a similar story. Though the orbital surface is rarely activated by cognitive demands—by making tasks more complex or difficult—it is often seen in studies of emotion or mood.[24] Again it seems that the lower parts of the frontal lobe—the orbital surface and the lower parts of the medial surface—are most important in social and emotional processes.

Otherwise, though, the strategy of dividing and conquering the frontal lobes proves tantalizing rather than compelling. Our best information comes from experiments in monkeys, comparing behavior after exact surgical removal of different parts of the frontal lobe. As I have described, there is a limit to how much can be learned from human brain damage. Damage is always dissimilar from one person to the next and rarely restricted to one anatomical or functional region. In monkey experiments, where removals are under the control of the experimenter, the evidence is much stronger. If definite functional separations exist between one brain area and another, this method should clearly show them. For most of the frontal lobe, however, this does not work very well. Many experiments, for example, have tried to separate the upper and lower parts of the lateral frontal surface. Sometimes there is a hint of a double dissociation. Task X is somewhat worse for animals with the upper part removed, and task Y somewhat worse for animals with the lower part removed. Usually, though, this hint occurs against a background impression that all the animals are impaired on all the tasks they are given. This is not a strong double dissociation—but it may be a strong clue to something. Though functional separations certainly exist within the frontal lobe, they do not look like hard differences between one specialized module and another. Instead they are blurry, or matters of degree. This is a clue I shall return to in chapter 6.

Here is another puzzle. Even when brain scans show that two patients have very similar damage, the effects on their behavior can be very different. One person is now living in the care of their partner, too disorganized to return to any kind of normal life. This person matches Luria's description. The other person has survived apparently unchanged. As Teuber put it: "Even with seemingly identical lesions, there often are quite unaccountable differences in . . . gross manifestations of frontal-lobe dysfunction, as if patients varied greatly in their tolerance for tissue loss from their frontal lobes."[25]

In the 1980s, when I first wanted to study frontal lobe patients, I was put into contact with one of the head neurosurgeons in the local Cambridge hospital. He was a typical, slightly starchy, somewhat amused elderly neurosurgeon with a lifetime of operations behind him. I told him about Luria and my ideas, and he said he would send some patients my way. He said he knew "just the people who would interest me." Well, the two people he sent me certainly were interesting. They both had very large removals; in both cases, more or less the whole of one frontal lobe had been taken out. I visited them in high excitement—my first frontal lobe patients—and gave them a list of tests designed to measure Spearman's g and Luria's impairments. Both of them were not just normal, they were supernormal, with Culture Fair IQs of perhaps 125 or more (I don't remember the exact numbers). In retrospect, I suspect that my neurosurgeon thought it would be entertaining—and perhaps even useful—if I was taught a bit of a lesson.

Though I have complained about how little we still know from our current work with frontal lobe patients, we do know that those two early patients were not representative. Usually, a large removal from the frontal lobe will produce quite a substantial fluid intelligence loss. But that is "usually." Sometimes it doesn't—and this is another clue I shall return to.

The chaotic world of frontal lobe patients points up an immense organizational challenge posed by each moment in our lives. In everything that we do, a complex structure of thought and action is used to make behavior useful—to achieve goals. By analogy with computer programs, I have called this structure a mental program. Assembling such programs depends on our massive store of world knowledge and on selecting just those things that, combined in the correct order, will move us from where we are to where we wish to be. In the frontal lobe patient, this active assembly process is impaired. Parts of the plan are left out; wrong parts intrude; essential knowledge is left out of consideration.

The evidence from functional MRI allows us to be more specific. In the multiple-demand regions of the frontal cortex, neural activity increases during any form of complex behavior. This makes these regions strong candidates for a role in the general disorganization of behavior that follows frontal lesions. This functional MRI evidence also suggests that the multiple-demand regions of the frontal lobe work together with an additional region further back in the brain, in a part of the parietal lobe.

I began this chapter with Spearman and Thomson and the question of what a test like Raven's Matrices actually measures. Does the brain contain an actual g process, or is g simply the average efficiency of all the brain's separate functions? The evidence now gives strong support to Spearman. This evidence suggests that such tests as Raven's Matrices indeed measure something specific: the mental programming functions of multiple-demand regions.

I said in chapter 2 that g is a valuable pointer. Now we can see where it points and what questions we must address. How are mental programs organized and assembled? How can this be controlled by many millions of separate, tiny neurons? What is special about the neurons of the frontal lobe? What happens in the brain as a mental program is run? These are no longer questions about what makes different people more or less "intelligent." They are questions about all of us.

They are questions, too, that require a different theoretical perspective. What exactly does it mean to talk about mental progams? What cognitive processes are required for intelligent mental programs to be built?

Chapter 5 **The Demystification of Thought**

t is time to return to the Cubans in their plaza. We saw earlier the power of the innate releasing mechanism, or IRM, in explaining animal behavior. As one IRM after another is triggered by its releasing conditions, a complex, goal-directed sequence of behavior is produced: the male stickleback attracts the female to mate, the toad approaches and eats the worm. Now it is time to consider our own sequences of goal-directed behavior: the fisherman steering his boat, the driver of the bicycle taxi adjusting his canopy. Here IRMs will not do—we need an equivalent idea that addresses the complexity and variety of human activity.

As a research student at the University of Oxford I spent a great deal of time measuring how quickly people can make simple decisions. In a typical experiment of this sort, a light appears at one of several positions on a computer screen, and the subject must choose which key to press in response. Various rules can define which response is correct. In one task, for example, there might be a row of four lights and a row of four keys. For each light, the correct response would be to press the spatially corresponding key (for example, leftmost key for leftmost light). In another task there could be the same lights and keys, but now the correct response to each light would be to press the opposite key in the row (for example, rightmost key for leftmost light). The time to choose the correct response can be measured as a function of various task manipulations. For example, each spatial transformation from stimulus to response position adds a certain time to the mental process; times increase with the number of possible stimuli and responses; times strongly depend on the predictability of events. (This is why those machines for measuring "reaction time" in British pubs are not very helpful for deciding whether a drinker should drive home. The reaction time measured by the machine, with a single, highly predictable stimulus and response, is completely different from the reaction time to address an unexpected traffic event.) By experiments of this sort, we hoped to understand the internal machinery of simple decisions. Certainly this approach allowed us to measure how quickly the machinery worked.

Though such experiments may be useful, they address a very restricted form of decision-making. A machine may be built to press one of four keys when one of four lights appears, but can a machine also be built for our everyday lives and the infinite variety of ill-specified, complex decisions that they entail? In Oxford I had two friends who had also been trained as psychologists, but in a more open, philosophical tradition. They were perennially unpersuaded that the science of psychology could ever make progress on real minds and real life. One weekend I had planned a trip to Manchester to visit my brother. My friends asked whether my kind of psychology could ever move from lights and buttons to the decision to travel to Manchester. We thought this was very funny; subsequently, we have always thought of it as the "travel to Manchester problem."

To my semiphilosopher friends, it seemed obvious that psychology could not really engage on the travel to Manchester problem. It seemed obvious that no mechanistic explanation could ever be given for the spontaneous decision to visit my brother, for choice of the weekend and the formulation of travel plans, for purchase of the train ticket and search for the correct station platform. To me it seemed equally obvious that all these problems were in principle quite soluble—indeed, that outlines of a solution were already available from the work that, since the mid-1950s, had been examining computers that thought.

A beautiful and fascinating example was the General Problem Solver, or GPS, of Allen Newell, Cliff Shaw, and Herbert Simon, a program that, toward the end of the 1950s, was already solving problems in symbolic logic.[1] Before programs like GPS, the world had been as my friends saw it, with human thought mysterious, unanalyzable, unique. After programs like GPS, the challenge of detailed explanation remained enormous, but the mystery had vanished. This was one of the grand moments for scientific understanding of the human mind. Describing an immediate precursor of GPS, Newell, Shaw, and Simon put it like this:

> It shows specifically and in detail how the processes that occur in human problem solving can be compounded out of elementary information processes, and hence how they can be carried out by mechanisms. . . . It shows that a program incorporating such processes, with appropriate organization, can in fact solve problems. This aspect of problem solving has been thought to be "mysterious" and unexplained because it was not understood how sequences of simple processes could account for the successful solution of complex problems. The theory dissolves the mystery by showing that nothing more need be added to the constitution of a successful problem solver.[2]

Fifty years later, something is still very striking. For much of what the brain does most naturally, computers remain hopelessly inadequate. So effortlessly that we imagine it must be easy, we see a visual world of trees jumbled one in front of another, birds flashing across, a friend approaching along a path, in the distance a brightly lit lake with boats. No computer can see like this . . . no computer can see anything like this. We listen to a story and, as the plot unfolds, understand the individual words, the meaning of the sentences, the whole world that the narrative gradually assembles. We think nothing of it, and again, it is not that computers cannot do this . . . it is that they seem light-years away from doing it.

Meanwhile, bizarrely, some of the tasks that are hardest for us suit the computer best. Most of us would struggle with the proofs of symbolic logic, yet when GPS generated those proofs, the way that it did this seemed immediately and naturally to be our way.

In the decades following GPS, its kind of "artificial intelligence" flourished. Mature versions give integrated explanations for many kinds of human thought, from chess to business decisions.[3] Toward the end of the twentieth century, though, this kind of thinking went rather out of fashion. The thought is that brains and computers, at least the conventional, digital computers used for programs like GPS, have quite different modes of operation. Brains solve their problems with networks of many millions of interconnected neurons, all acting in parallel, simultaneously influencing and being influenced by many others. As we can see from their success in problems such as vision and language understanding, this mode of operation must be extremely powerful. It allows brains to do things quite outside the capability of any current machine; many of its principles must still be quite outside current understanding. In contrast, conventional digital computers solve problems by a series of elementary steps performed one after the other. It is this series of steps that we call a "program." As science has begun to engage on the massively parallel action of neurons in the brain, the serial programs of conventional computers have increasingly been sidelined as poor models of the mind.

In my opinion, this line of thinking leads us badly astray. Perhaps there is a good reason why computers see so poorly but think so well. Perhaps this contrast is actually a clue to different kinds of brain operation.

So what are the principles of thinking computers? We can begin with the idea of *goals*—of processes coordinated to produce a constant, desired outcome.

In early experimental psychology, behavior was often conceived in terms of stimulus and response. Ivan Pavlov's experiments with dogs are an early and well-known example. After learning that a bell signals the imminent arrival of food, dogs will salivate in response to the sound of the bell, suggesting a new link between a stimulus (the bell) and a response (salivation). From these small beginnings, the idea of stimulus-response links expanded until, by the early 1950s, it dominated much thinking in psychology. Elaborate theoretical structures attempted to explain how stimulus-response learning could underlie much, even all of animal and human behavior.

To think of the problem this way, however, leaves something out. Responses in general are not just fixed movements, such as a contraction of the salivary glands or the press of a rat's paw on a lever. Instead, behavior has a *purpose*. It acts to achieve a constant end, and though the effects of real movements may vary, a structure of behavior is continued until the constant end is produced.

A brilliant exposition of this point was made in one of the founding books of modern psychology, *Plans and the Structure of Behavior*, published by George Miller, Eugene Galanter, and Karl Pribram in 1960.[4] For Miller, Galanter, and Pribram, the fundamental unit of behavior was no longer the stimulus-response link. Instead it was what they called a TOTE unit, standing for test-operate-test-exit. TOTE units transform behavior from isolated stimuli and responses into organized structures; specifically, structures for achieving goals. The principle of the TOTE unit could apply to all kinds of behavior and thought, from the longest-term goals of pursuing a career to the shortest-term goals of entering a room or turning on the light. To illustrate, Miller, Galanter, and Pribram used the example of hammering a nail into a plank of wood.

The nail is a good example because, in general, its response to being hit is unpredictable. It will not do to see a nail standing out of a piece of wood and simply to hit it a fixed number of times. Instead, you hit it until it is in. Miller, Galanter, and Pribram accordingly suggested that behavior is controlled like this:

> TEST: Is the nail down?
> IF NO, OPERATE: Hit the nail and return to TEST
> IF YES, EXIT (goal achieved)

Because each OPERATE is followed by a further TEST, the TOTE unit cycles through a loop of operations until the goal is achieved. It is a structure built to produce a constant outcome. It is immediately obvious, furthermore, that the idea is right—that this is exactly how we actually do hammer in nails.

Miller, Galanter, and Pribram went on to make another point. TOTE units have a natural way of stacking up in a hierarchy, extending the explanation of behavior both upward and downward in complexity. Let's name them by their TESTS, so that the above unit becomes the "Nail down?" unit. Consider its OPERATE stage. It has two obvious phases: the hammer is raised, then the nail is struck. Now we can imagine two further TOTE units, one for each phase. In the first:

TEST: Is the hammer raised?

IF NO, OPERATE: Lift the hammer upward and return to TEST

IF YES, EXIT

In the second:

TEST: Has the hammer struck the nail?

IF NO, OPERATE: Strike

IF YES, EXIT

Now, we have three TOTE units, one at the higher level ("Nail down?") and two at the lower ("Hammer up?" and "Nail struck?"). The OPERATE stage of the "Nail down?" unit passes control to the lower level. The "Hammer up?" TOTE operates until the hammer is up. (Note again the advantage of operating until a fixed result is achieved. For example, the hammer may be heavier than anticipated or may hit an obstacle on the way up, but the TOTE operates until the goal is achieved and the hammer is in a position to strike.) When the "Hammer up?" TOTE has its test satisfied, control is passed to the "Nail struck?" TOTE. Completion of its test also completes the OPERATE stage of the higher-level unit, "Nail down?" This unit proceeds to its own test ("Nail down?"), and the whole process either recycles or exits.

In the TOTE conception, behavior is not controlled in simple stimulus-response pairs. Instead, control is in triples of current state (the position of the nail), goal state (nail hammered flush), and action (hammering). A series of actions is chosen in a highly specific way. It is chosen so that the difference between current and goal states is reduced until the goal itself is achieved.

A few moments' thought shows that this general picture recurs in all that we do, from the simplest, most habitual actions to the highest-level plans. At work and in our relationships we may set goals that extend over years or decades and assiduously operate under their control until either they are achieved, or abandoned, or time just runs out. On a shopping trip we set goals that last over minutes or hours. But even just changing gear in the car, we move the gearshift from third to second *until we feel that it has clicked into place;* entering a room in the dark, we feel for the light switch *until our hand makes contact,* and we press *until the light comes on.* Though sometimes we say that one person is more "goal-directed" than another, in the sense of the TOTE unit we are all completely goal-directed, all the time.

The TOTE unit is a relatively simple conception and captures a simple behavioral fact. The hammer example is highly informative but leaves many questions unanswered. For example, we assumed a certain flow of control from one TOTE unit to another, but how is this flow of control achieved? How is it established for behavior that is not simple and well-learned but complex and novel? Now we move from one fragment of well-learned behavior to complex goal-directed thought, and to the operation of programs like Newell, Shaw, and Simon's General Problem Solver/GPS and its many descendants.

To illustrate we will use the problem that GPS was first designed to solve, finding proofs in symbolic logic. The basic elements of this task, which Newell, Shaw, and Simon gave both to GPS and to human problem solvers, are letters and connectors joining them. There are four connectors:

- meaning *and*
∨ meaning *or*
⊃ meaning *implies*
~ meaning *not*

Now the program/subject is given two expressions, for example:

$$R \cdot (\sim P \supset Q)$$
$$(Q \vee P) \cdot R$$

The problem is to prove the second expression starting from the first. A bit of thought shows that the first expression does indeed imply the second: If R and "not P implies Q" are both true (first expression), then "Q or P" and R are also both true (second expression). It takes some thought, though in fact it is one of the easiest problems, used in the study as a practice item.

To solve any problem, the first thing a program needs is *knowledge*. To speak of a computer's having knowledge may at first seem strange, but its meaning is relatively straightforward. Inside a computer, of course, there are no actual letters or words, but a computer knows your address because it can print it on a screen when asked. In other words, a sequence of operations has been set up so that, when a person types the question, "What is the address for this credit card number?" the correct sequence of letters and numbers is returned onto the screen. Inside the computer, there may be nothing but strings of os and 1s (not really even os and 1s, but just some physical realization of two alternative states that we can imagine as os and 1s), but written in the right way, and interpreted by the right program, these can be used to store and produce any kind of knowledge of the world. Inside us, similarly, there may be nothing but billions of neurons firing impulses and rules for connecting one neuron to the next, but asked in the right way, we, too, can respond to the question, "What is the square root of 4?" with the answer, "2." The physical devices may be different, but the general principle is the same: to operate usefully in the world, the first thing we need is *knowledge*, knowledge of the facts and rules that bear on that aspect of the world we are addressing.

For GPS, then, the first thing was to equip it with knowledge of facts that bear on problems in symbolic logic. One sort of knowledge concerned the expressions themselves; the program recorded the content of expressions, with their letters, parentheses, and connectors, much as a modern computer stores a credit card number. More important were rules that allowed one expression to be translated into another. In the work of Newell, Shaw, and Simon, neither the computer nor the human subjects actually knew the meaning of the connectors—they were not told that that · means *and* or that ⊃ means *implies*. Instead, as in conventional logical proofs, the program/subject was simply given a set of rules that could be used to transform one string into another. The problem was to find the series of transformations that began with the starting string and ended with the target string.

Both computer and subject had twelve rules (Rs) available. Below are three that I shall need to illustrate GPS at work:

R1. A · B → B · A
    A ∨ B → B ∨ A

The arrow means that you are permitted to transform the first string into the second. You can see that this rule expresses a basic logical necessity: If A and B are both true, then we can also state that B and A are both true; if A is true or B is true, we can also state that B is true or A is true. Remember, though, that for computer/subject, the meaning of · and ∨ were not given, so R1 was just a rule defining one allowable way to transform expressions. If the connector was · or ∨, the computer/subject could swap which letter came first.

The next rule is:

R5. A ∨ B ↔ ~ (~ A · ~ B)

↔ means that the rule can be used in both directions. Again you can see that the rule fits logic: If A or B is true, then "not A" and "not B" cannot both be true.

Last we will need:

R6. A ⊃ B ↔ ~ A ∨ B

If A implies B, then either "not A" or "B."

We can see that, without knowledge of the world and how it works, there would be no way for problem solving to proceed. In our own minds, of course, there is a vast store of knowledge bearing on many different problems, many varied aspects of the world. We know not just about transformation rules in symbolic logic but about our homes, our families, arithmetic, world history, how to catch a bus, the songs of Joni Mitchell, the Internet, the many millions of facts, rules, and experiences we have accumulated over our lifetime. In psychology, a distinction is often drawn between two kinds of knowledge of the world: semantic memory, which stores general facts, and episodic memory, which stores individual experiences.[5] For our purposes, though, the distinction does not really matter. Both kinds of memory provide information that potentially can be useful in problem solving. Here we can bundle them under the general name long-term memory.

Now we can examine a trace of GPS at work on the simple problem described above. It must navigate a path through its twelve possible rules, starting with the first expression and ending with the second. This is not easy to do; I have given you just the rules you need, plus one other, and even so, it probably takes some thought to find the correct path. With all twelve rules, it would take a lot more thought. GPS thought like this:

First, it noted *differences* between the start and end expressions. This strongly recalls the TOTE unit. GPS was deciding how the goal state differs from the current state. It thought in terms of several rather simple kinds of differences, such as a difference in letters, a difference in connectors, a difference in position.

Second, it knew a list of the differences that each rule might help with. For example, R1 helps with a difference in position, whereas R5 helps with a difference in connectors.

Third, it selected rules relevant to each difference. It found the difference between the current state and the goal state, and it chose rules that were plausible candidates to reduce that difference. This basic idea is called means-ends analysis and is perhaps the fundamental idea in a system that can produce any kind of goal-directed behavior.

So, the starting expression is R · (~ P ⊃ Q); the expression to be produced is (Q ∨ P) · R. The overall goal is to transform the first into the second. Here is one GPS run.[6]

First, GPS notes the difference in position. The R is to the left in the start expression but to the right in the goal expression. This is one problem that needs to be fixed. GPS sets up a subgoal: to exchange the two sides. Examining its twelve rules, it determines that R1 is relevant for differences in position. It chooses this rule to apply, producing

(~ P ⊃ Q) · R

So far so good—this is certainly closer to the goal, with the R on the right—but now there are more complex differences to eliminate. In the left half of the new expression that has been achieved is a connector that differs from the goal connector. Eliminating this difference is established as a new subgoal. Because several rules change connectors, GPS has to make a guess. Its first guess is an attempt to transform (~ P ⊃ Q) using R5.

This throws up an immediate problem. Though R5 changes connectors, (~ P ⊃ Q) is not in the right form for R5 to apply. To resolve this difficulty, GPS sets up yet another subgoal. Now it wants to transform (~ P ⊃ Q) into a form fitting R5. After a number of failed attempts, it abandons R5 and makes another guess.

The next guess is R6. R6 applies, producing $(\sim \sim P \vee Q)$. A further relevant piece of knowledge is that two "nots" cancel; accordingly $\sim \sim P$ is the same as P and we have $(P \vee Q)$. Suddenly things are looking much better. All that is left to do is to detect one remaining difference in position, this time just in the left half of the expression; set up a final subgoal to remove this difference; use R1 again; and write QED.

If you tried to solve the problem yourself, it is probably already obvious that what you did was very much what GPS did. You may not have made the poor choice of R5, especially not without the other nine rules to distract you, but with enough rules to choose from and with problems that required longer sets of transformations, there would certainly be cases of trying and finally rejecting possible routes. GPS, of course, did not just solve this easy problem; by the same general process of means-ends analysis, it was able to solve much more difficult problems, too. And when it did so, the protocols it produced were much like the protocols of human subjects thinking aloud as they worked on the same problems. Like GPS, the human subjects also focused on specific changes that needed to be made, searched for rules that might help with those changes, tried out and rejected possible candidates. Through the general process of means-ends analysis, a complex, sometimes branching path was generated, leading away from the initial state in search of the final goal.

There is something important hidden in the thought path of GPS, a feature that has turned out to be essential in any problem-solving program of this sort. The computer actually has two kinds of memory: its long-term knowledge of the world and its short-term representation of the current problem. The program does not just need to know the rules of symbolic logic; at each moment of a solution, it needs to know what expression it has currently generated, what subgoal it may be working on, what final goal it is approaching, and so on. This second kind of memory is now usually called working memory. It is like a blackboard for writing temporary results—everything the program needs to know about where it is right now.

The solution path of GPS makes a second important point. This is how easy it is, at any stage of problem solving, to go wrong. In part, this is a matter of how well the knowledge is organized. With a better procedure for choosing candidate rules, for example, GPS might never have tried R5; instead, seeing a better match to the connectors in its current expression, it might have gone straight to R6. Another important factor is how much knowledge the program has to search. Even twelve rules are much harder than three, and in our own memories, the search problem must be staggering. The general point is that, no matter how well the system is designed, the correct path may not be easy to find—even when, in a sense, the program's knowledge does contain the answer. Just as we see in our own problem solving, wrong paths may be taken, dead ends explored. At every step is another chance for progress to be derailed.

The symbolic logic problem is rather abstract. At first sight, it may seem that a program like GPS is suitable only for abstract problems of this sort, with a small, fixed set of possible moves, applied in a highly confined world of symbols. Very much the same principles, however, can be used to address much more concrete, real-life problems. In these we may be concerned not just with thought but with real action; whereas some moves of the program change just the task or world description in working memory, others are physical actions, such as hammering a nail. Similarly, the model of the current situation (the description in working memory) is built up not just from knowledge in long-term memory but from facts simultaneously delivered by the senses. Now there is all the flexibility of real, concrete interaction with a real, physical, and often unpredictable world.

To illustrate we will consider computer and human protocols for a much more lifelike shopping task, taken from the work of Barbara and Frederick Hayes-Roth.[7] Now the problem is very different from symbolic logic, the knowledge is different, the possible moves are different. Still, the general principles are the same, and once again, the work of Hayes-Roth and Hayes-Roth showed how computers and people working on the same problems generated very much the same solutions.

This time the problem was to plan a day in town. It began like this:

> You have just finished working out at the health club. It is 11:00 and you can plan the rest of your day as you like. However, you must pick up your car from the Maple Street parking garage by 5:30 and then head home. You'd also like to see a movie today, if possible. Show times at both movie theatres are 1:00, 3:00, and 5:00. Both movies are on your "must see" list, but go to whichever one most conveniently fits into your plan. Your other errands are as follows:
> • pick up medicine for your dog at the vet;
> • buy a fan belt for your refrigerator at the appliance store;
> • check out two of the three luxury apartments;
> • meet a friend for lunch at one of the restaurants;
> • . . . .

The complete list of additional errands was even longer, so that there was no possible way for everything to be fit in. In addition to the list of errands, the computer/subject was given a map showing the layout of the town, the locations of the stores and movie theaters, and so on. Of course, the computer simply planned the route and did not actually go shopping, and in the experiment itself, it was the same for the human subjects. It is obvious, however, that the same principles could be applied to real, physical shopping—or to any other real expedition in a complex, novel world.

The protocols of real subjects showed very much what you might expect. Because there was no way to complete everything, subjects needed to prioritize: organizing the list of errands into essentials and secondaries. Now with a list of essentials, they began to search outward from the starting location at the health club, trying to find other important errands nearby. Usually, they began to notice areas of town where many errands were clustered. They began formulating a plan around going to that general area and knocking off all the errands in a group, all the while remembering the time constraints of meeting the friend for lunch and reaching the parking garage at 5:30 p.m.

This is not symbolic logic, but the general principles are very similar. There is a set of goals, and there are moves that can be made to reach those goals. Long-term knowledge is used to rank the importance of different goals and to suggest important constraints on the solution—for example, the advantage of finding a cluster of errands that can all be done together. Working memory is used to keep track of the plan as it evolves—that we have just bought the dog's medicine on Oak Street and are now searching for other important errands on the way to the next area of town. Gradually, a sequence of moves is built up—now, physical moves across the map—each moving toward the achievement of goals and subgoals.

The plans of human subjects fit this general picture, and equipped with the right knowledge—the right understanding of which errands were more and less important, a procedure for finding spatial clusters, the map, knowledge of durations and times—the program of Hayes-Roth and Hayes-Roth did much the same. The computer's final day plan and route were perhaps a little better than a real person's; the computer was less optimistic in trying to squeeze too much in. Neither human nor computer generated perfect routes. Just like GPS choosing R5, there would be places where the wrong errand was chosen next, so that later the route had to detour to pick up something essential that had been missed. Still, with the right knowledge, the same list of goals, and the general strategy of choosing moves that bring a goal closer, both human and computer generated perfectly reasonable day plans, ones you might recognize as your own.

In the real world, planning is perhaps more chaotic than it is in symbolic logic. In both human and computer solutions to the errands task, current plans were often overturned as new considerations arose. The person/computer might be heading down Belmont Street, notice the department store and realize that, by cutting through it, they could get to a newsstand and pick up a previously unplanned secondary, a gardening magazine to be purchased. Compared to symbolic logic, the real world has many more options to consider, many more possible forks in the route. This does not seem to call, though, for any new general principle—just more complex knowledge and more complex methods of navigation.

The above examples show something of the power of artificial intelligence. They show how computer programs, equipped with detailed knowledge of the world, can produce complex, useful, goal-directed thought and behavior. They show that the way these computers think looks very much the same as the way we ourselves think. The protocols generated by the program—the avenues that are explored, the ideas that are generated—remind us forcibly and repeatedly of ourselves. Why? What general principle is involved?

The answer is related to the question I asked at the start of this chapter: why conventional digital computers, with their mode of sequential rather than parallel operation, are so well suited to thought and problem solving while at the same time so poorly suited to many other kinds of brain operation. The answer is also well captured in remarks that Newell, Shaw, and Simon themselves made about their work. As quoted earlier, one of their earliest insights was that complex problems must be solved by concatenating solutions to simpler subproblems, that "sequences of simple processes could account for the successful solution of complex problems."[8]

In problem solving of this sort, the essential move is to find a way that the entire problem—the problem defined by the mismatch between the current state and the final goal state—can be split into useful steps or parts, such that the parts can be solved in turn, and when all these solutions have been found, the whole problem will also have been solved.

It is obvious that everything we do in fact has this structure. To travel to work, we solve subproblems of finding our car keys, inserting them into the car door, getting our body into the driving seat, and many more. Just as in the TOTE system, each of these subproblems can be further divided into subproblems of its own: remembering where we last put down the car keys, navigating to that place, directing our eyes and hand, and so on. The whole problem is solved by finding natural parts—subproblems that can be solved individually, without undue dependence on the rest of the structure—and addressing these parts in sequence.

We can also see why problems have to be broken down in this way. Generally speaking, a high-level goal will not on its own trigger any very specific action. Before real actions can be selected, the goal will have to be decomposed, adding more constraints to the solution. Suppose that you have chosen to make soup for dinner. What should you do with your left hand? At present you cannot possibly answer that question, but if you add a subgoal of chopping onions, an onion on the chopping board in front of you, and the knowledge that a chopping knife is available on the wall rack to the left, now you can proceed to reach out and take it. The point is beautifully made in an early computer simulation by Earl Sacerdoti.[9] The robot controlled by this program inhabited a building composed of several rooms and connecting doors. It could be given such tasks as: starting in room X, proceed to room Z, collecting an object A from room Y on the way. Working simply from the final goal—robot in room Z, accompanied by object A—the program created chaotic behavior. The robot might finally solve the problem, but only after much wandering around different rooms and through different doors. At each stage, there were simply too many possibilities to consider. Things proceeded very differently when the system was allowed to produce subgoals for the robot: to travel first to room Y, to reach the door of the current room, and so on. Now the final goal led to the choice of subgoals, and the subgoals controlled the details of movement. Now navigation was excellent, with subgoals traversed in turn to the final destination.

In each part of a problem's solution, a small amount of knowledge is assembled for solution of just a restricted subproblem. We might call this assembly a cognitive *enclosure*—a mental epoch in which, for as long as it takes, just a small subproblem is addressed, and just those facts bearing on this subproblem are allowed into consideration. Effective thought and action require that problems be broken down into useful cognitive enclosures, discovered and executed in turn. As each enclosure is completed, it must deliver important results to the next stage, then relinquish its control of the system and disappear.

Equipped with this general view of thought, we can address a range of intriguing questions. In each case, apparently mysterious issues are illuminated by the idea of decomposing problems and assembling successive cognitive enclosures toward a final complete solution.

First is the question of *insight*. We admire few things in the human mind as strongly as the moment of insight, the flash of sudden understanding. We tell stories of scientists whose insight came in a dream of a snake eating its tail or as a violent interruption of a bath. It is often thought that a computer can never show insight—a computer can only follow rules, as specified in advance by its program.

Some of our most appealing observations of insight come not from humans but from chimpanzees. They are described in *The Mentality of Apes*, a book published in German by Wolfgang Köhler in 1917 and translated into English in 1925.[10] During World War I, Köhler was director of the Prussian Academy of Sciences Anthropoid Station on Tenerife. He devoted his time to studying a group of chimpanzees kept captive at the station for study of their mental capacities.

At the time of Köhler's work, experimental psychology was dominated by studies of rather mindless animal learning. Cats or dogs might be placed in an apparatus where some hidden mechanism produced an unexpected benefit; for example, pressing a lever might deliver a morsel of food, or releasing a catch might allow the animal to escape. In such experiments, the observation was that animals learned by trial and error, by chance finally happening on the correct behavior and then, through repetition, stamping it in. Such observations were raised to the status of presumed laws of animal behavior. In retrospect, one may wonder what else an animal could have done when faced with an apparatus of this sort, controlled by a hidden, arbitrary mechanism unrelated to any other aspect of the animal's experience. In the real world of the chimpanzee compound, populated by familiar objects and familiar kinds of problems, Köhler made a set of very different observations.

Here is a typical example. Koko has been tied up near a wall; suspended high up the wall is a piece of fruit. A box sits on the ground nearby. Köhler describes Koko's behavior:

> He jumped upwards several times to begin with . . . could not reach
> so far, and then turned away from the wall, after a variety of such
> actions, but without noticing the box. He appeared to have given up

his efforts, but always returned to them from time to time. After some time, on turning away from the wall, his eye fell on the box: he approached it, *looked straight towards the objective*, and gave the box a slight push, which did not, however, move it; his movements had grown much slower; he left the box standing, took a few paces away from it, but at once returned, and pushed it again and *again with his eyes on the objective*, but quite gently, and not as though he really intended to alter its position. He turned away again, turned back at once, and gave the box a third tentative shove, after which he again moved slowly about. . . . The objective was rendered more tempting by the addition of a piece of orange (the *non plus ultra* of delight!), and in a few seconds Koko was once more at the box, seized it, dragged it in one movement almost up to a point directly beneath the objective . . . mounted it, and tore down the fruit. . . . [F]rom the beginning, Koko showed a lively interest in the fruit, but none— at first—in the box, and when he began to move the latter he did not appear *apathetic* but *uncertain*: there is only one (colloquial) expression that really fits his behaviour at that juncture: "it's beginning to dawn on him!"[11]

Köhler's book is a delight, describing many similar moments of insight in the life of his chimpanzees. In flashes of understanding, the animals realize that they can get food from outside the cage by dragging it in with a stick; or reach bananas suspended from the ceiling by balancing a loose stick and climbing it like a combination of vaulting pole and ladder; or pull a string that passes over the branch of a tree to bring down a hanging treat. In all these cases, Köhler describes the beautiful moment of the new idea, as uncertainty and frustration are replaced by vivid understanding and a sudden path to solution.

Later, Köhler's followers examined very similar phenomena in human subjects. Two ropes hang from the ceiling.[12] The subject is asked to tie them together, but they are just too far apart to grab one

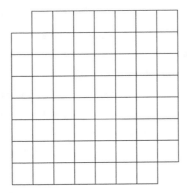

Figure 7. The Kaplan and Simon
insight problem.

and then reach for the other. An impasse. Apparently by chance, the experimenter knocks into one rope and starts it swinging. The swinging rope gives the subject a simple idea. . . .

What do such moments of insight mean? How might they be understood in terms of a thinking computer, solving its problems by a series of small, focused cognitive enclosures? To think about this we can consider an insight problem studied by Craig Kaplan and Herbert Simon—the same Simon who was among the original creators of GPS and a founding father of artificial intelligence.[13]

Imagine that you are given a board divided into sixty-four (eight-by-eight) small squares (fig. 7). The top left and the bottom right squares have been removed. You also have thirty-one dominoes, each big enough to cover two squares. Either show how the dominoes can be arranged to cover the remaining sixty-two squares, or prove that this cannot be done.

The first move is perhaps to imagine a possible solution. Starting at the right, dominoes are mentally placed along the bottom row, but reaching the end, one square is left, and so a domino must be placed vertically. Now a second row can be added along the top on the first, but since one square was taken up at the left by the vertical domino, one square now remains uncovered on the right, and a second vertical domino must be used. When the strategy continues to the top of the board, it finally fails . . . but what has been learned? Is the problem impossible, or was this arrangement just not the right one?

So, a different arrangement might be tried. You can imagine several for yourself, all equally unsuccessful. Perhaps you may begin to suspect that the problem really is impossible, but that is a far cry from proving it. Like Koko, all you sense is uncertainty . . . a sense that the answer must be there but that you just can't see it.

In this form, in fact, Kaplan and Simon found that almost nobody can solve the problem. An engineering student in their study spent eighteen hours and filled sixty-one pages of a notebook in an unsuccessful search for the solution; rather winningly, Kaplan and Simon describe the Herculean persistence of their colleague Allen Newell, another of the creators of GPS, exhaustively examining the thousands of ways in which the dominoes can be arranged. People resort to complex arithmetical calculations, abstract descriptions of possible relations between pairs of squares, and many other plans of attack. With all of this work, the solution seems no closer.

All of this, meanwhile, follows very much the scheme we discussed in GPS and its descendants. Many attempts are made to find a series of moves that successfully approaches the goal. The moves may be of many different kinds . . . imaginary placement of dominoes, abstract geometrical analyses, and so on. Many cognitive enclosures are formed and assembled into possible routes to a solution. None of these routes proves effective.

In the next stage of the experiment, Kaplan and Simon began to give hints. Here is the first: Imagine that the squares are colored black and white, as if on a chessboard. This hint on its own is still not usually enough, so the subject can be further encouraged to "think about the colors." By now, some subjects start to see a solution, though it is likely still to take several minutes.

Here is the final hint: Consider that each domino covers one black and one white square. Now consider that the two squares removed had the same color. A problem that was impossible to solve is now absurdly easy. There is a moment of insight.

As Kaplan and Simon put it, and as we saw already in GPS, problem solving is a question of *search*. In the knowledge store of a computer— and even more in our own, vast store of world knowledge—many facts are known that might bear on the current problem. These include the spatial layout of the squares, the size of the dominoes, the number of squares remaining, and much more. So many facts offer many possible paths to pursue in the search for a solution—in the construction of sequences of moves that attempt to reach the goal. The whole trick is to find the *right* facts: the fact that a box can be stood on, that a string can be pulled, that a domino must always cover one black and one white square. With the right description of the situation—with the right cognitive enclosure—the path to solution is suddenly clear. The moment of insight occurs.

In fact, Kaplan and Simon did not trouble actually to build a computer simulation of the chessboard problem. In a way, there is no point. Once the process has been conceived in the above way, it is obvious that a computer could be made to follow the same unsuccessful paths as the human problem solver, and encouraged by hints, finally to find the right description and the right path. As in so many cases of artificial intelligence, once the thinking process is properly described, the mystery disappears.

There is a popular myth that human beings "typically use no more than 10 percent of their brains." I have no idea how this myth originated, though modern brain imaging tells if anything the opposite story. What is really most remarkable is how even the simplest tasks, such as pressing a button when a target stimulus appears, engage so much of the brain. What is true, however, is the essence of the cognitive enclosure. At any given moment, we take into consideration only a tiny fraction of the total available knowledge in our brains. For eighteen hours, the engineering student knew that every domino must cover two adjacent squares and could certainly have explained that, if these squares were alternately black and white, each domino would cover one of each. This knowledge was always in principle available . . . a system capable of checking all possible knowledge, all possible routes to solution, would have found it immediately. Our system, however, is not built that way. Instead the knowledge—almost all of the knowledge that we have—lies dormant until it enters the current path, the current series of cognitive enclosures. The trick of problem solving is to find the right knowledge—to divide the problem into just the right subproblems and in this way to navigate the right path to solution.

Central to human intelligence is the power of *abstraction*. We see abstract ideas, abstract reasoning as fundamental in all arenas of human thought—in philosophy, science, mathematics, art. What does abstraction mean, and how does it relate to the ideas captured in GPS and its descendants?

Even before the development of computer intelligence, many of the fundamental ideas behind programs like GPS were laid out in a monograph, "On Problem Solving," published by Karl Duncker in 1945.[14] Like Newell, Shaw, and Simon, Duncker saw problem solving as the discovery of a path linking the "given situation" to the "goal situation." He grasped the essential importance of shaping the solution by discovery of useful subgoals, each establishing its own, separate subproblem for solution. He also used the same sort of protocol analysis that we have seen in later problem-solving studies, asking subjects to think aloud as they worked their way to the solution. One of Duncker's favorite problems was based on use of X-rays to destroy a stomach tumor. Subjects were instructed that X-rays would destroy any tissue that they encountered. This applied equally to the tumor and to the healthy tissue surrounding it. The problem was how to destroy the tumor while leaving healthy tissue unharmed.

For this task, Duncker obtained many hours of protocols generated by subjects thinking aloud as they worked. By analysis of these protocols, he came to an interesting conclusion. Usually, he proposed, the full solution was shaped by a realization of what he called its "functional value"—the abstract principle by which it worked. Once the principle was derived, different attempts could be made to achieve the same general end. In this way, the abstract principle guides reasoning to the ultimate solution. It is like Sacerdoti's program, guiding its path through the building by first deciding to reach the door of the starting room, or like the many subgoals set up to shape the solutions of GPS.

For example, in the X-ray problem, subjects might produce the functional principle of avoiding contact between rays and healthy tissue. Several attempts might be made to achieve this same general end: directing rays down the esophagus, operating to expose the tumor, and so on. A second principle might be desensitizing the healthy tissue; subjects might propose chemical injections or warm-up doses of radiation. A third principle was to increase the intensity of rays at the point of the tumor. Variants included somehow turning up the power at the moment the tumor was reached, using lenses, and the best solution, sending narrow beams from several directions at once, intersecting at the tumor site. In all these cases, solutions can be grouped by the abstract principle they share.

In fact, Köhler in his studies of chimpanzees had already made similar observations. Once a chimp had learned to drag food into the cage using a stick, the discovery was generalized to many other objects—drinking bowls, hats, and many other things could also be used as tools to extend the arm and bring a desired object into reach. As in the case of Duncker's "functional value," the chimpanzee had learned an abstract principle. The same theme is echoed in Kaplan and Simon's studies of the chessboard problem, where successful subjects were likely to mention "invariants," or abstract aspects of the problem, on their way to a discovery of the critical invariant ("all possible arrangements of dominoes will cover equal numbers of black and white squares") and the final solution.

So what is an abstract idea, a functional value, an invariant? An abstraction is something that applies over many individual cases—a property of these cases that remains true even as other things vary. In problem solving, it is a property of the solution that can be fixed *while many other parts of the solution are still unknown*. It is a part that can be worked on independently of others. We are back again to the idea of a cognitive enclosure—to discovery of how a problem can be broken into usefully separate parts, and the whole solution built out of concatenated part-solutions. The essence of abstraction is again the power of cognitive focus—of admitting into consideration just one feature of the problem, one aspect of relevant world knowledge, and using the implications of this one feature to direct useful thought and conclusions.

In programs like GPS, what is simulated is a chain of inference. At each step, new features can be added to working memory. The new feature can be a conclusion implied by the current state: "Given that X is true, Y must also be true"; or it can be a subgoal that would aid achievement of the goal: "If we could do X, we would be a step closer to Y." Knowledge of the world is used to extract *implications*: If X therefore Y.

We are familiar, of course, with the idea of thought as a chain of inference. Proving that two triangles are congruent, we proceed by proving that two angles are the same. The identity of these angles then can be used to prove that two other angles must also be the same, and so on. In chess, we consider that, if we make move X, our opponent will be obliged to make move Y. Following move Y, the board will be in state Z, and so on. Sherlock Holmes and Hercule Poirot astonish their readers by the same means, drawing a chain of implications from the absence of a set of keys or a dog's failure to bark.

A chain of inference is invaluable, but it carries risks. The difficulty is that, in the real world, many of our "implications" come with an implied probability: X may probably imply Y, but in making this inference, there is some possibility that we are wrong. Chaining makes this especially dangerous because of the way that probabilities multiply.

Suppose that, in a chain of reasoning, the probability that each step is correct is 0.9. This may sound quite reassuring, but suppose now that the chain of inference has ten steps of this sort. If two steps each have a probability correct of 0.9, the probability that both are correct— the first is correct and then the second is also correct—is 0.9^2, or 0.81. For ten steps in a row, the probability that the final conclusion is correct has sunk to 0.9^{10}, or 0.35. The laws of probability imply that, unless each inference is perfect, long chains of reasoning will often drift off course. At some point along the chain, the wrong conclusion will be drawn, and the whole process be led astray.

This thought perhaps explains why, in real life, there are few cases of brilliant detectives revealing astonishing conclusions. Quite rightly, we tend to limit ourselves to the most obvious, easily derived conclusions, because in our real lives, there is little that follows with a probability of 1.0 from the fact that the dog did not bark.

The same considerations show why mathematics has such power—why it can be used to derive astonishing conclusions, such as the conclusion that $E = mc^2$, or that the universe expanded from a microscopic initial state. In the world of mathematical relations, implications really do come with a probability of 1.0. The expression $2 + 2$ does not probably equal 4, it certainly equals 4, and if we use this rule, we will *never* be led astray. This means that we can add two numbers, or ten, or a thousand, and provided that we use the rules correctly, the final sum is guaranteed to be correct. There is no error and therefore no concatenation of error as the chain of steps is assembled.

A similar principle explains the obsession with minutiae that so often seems typical of experimental science. Essential to science are observations made with sufficient care that the conclusions drawn really are true. Though scientists may often seem comical in their tiny steps made in tiny, arcane corners of knowledge, small steps have a big advantage. The boldness comes not in the single, carefully tested step but in the accurate course finally plotted into new, often unimagined territory.

In programs like GPS, essentially the same mechanisms produce sequences of thought and sequences of behavior. It is the same machine that derives a geometrical proof or that navigates its owner out of the house, into the car, and off to work. Interestingly, the risks of a chain of inference may be much less in real activity, because very often, the real world immediately tells us when the path is lost. In leaving the house, you do not simply infer that the car keys are in the desk drawer: You approach the drawer, and if the keys are not there, the plan is rethought. Now it does not matter that the whole path for reaching work has many steps, each with some probability of unpredictable failure; when failure is encountered, it is likely to be immediately detected and corrected. Again, this strongly recalls the power of experimental science; long routes can be pursued with confidence as long as constant checks can be made for error.

❖

Can a computer ever be spontaneous? Can it decide, as we can, to break off from its current line of thought and pursue some different goal? Can it elect one weekend not to stay home and play cricket but to visit its brother in Manchester?

At first sight, it seems that a program like GPS can never do more than solve the problems it is given: to prove the particular theorem that the programmer types in as a goal. In the early years of artificial intelligence, indeed, this kind of criticism was often directed at problem-solving programs. A little more thought, however, suggests that the architecture of a system like GPS already implies the solution. Already, the program works flexibly to generate different possible lines of action in the restricted context it has been given. Increasing this flexibility is simply a matter of broadening the context.

An element of this was already evident in the shopping task of Hayes-Roth and Hayes-Roth. With multiple goals, and multiple routes available to navigate to those goals, a program's plan can abruptly change direction, as a new consideration comes to attention. The program may be approaching the veterinarian's office, but as it passes the florist, the program suddenly suspends its current goal and decides to make a quick stop. Circumstances change as the plan evolves, and as the contents of working memory change, some new possible line of action is suggested. More generally, all problem-solving programs must be equipped with methods to evaluate the relative merits of many possible lines of action. Subgoals are chosen, and new cognitive enclosures are created, not just at random, but because the program's knowledge suggests that they are desirable. In the focused world of proving a theorem in formal logic, "desirability" may be defined simply in terms of approach to the proof, but in the real world, the program must weigh many aspects of desirability. In the world of Hayes-Roth and Hayes-Roth, desirability must be compared for shopping, lunch, a visit to the vet. The importance of different goals is combined with the current state—the current time, the current position on the map—to choose what should be done next. In our own much more complex world, we are free at any moment to abandon the current line of action for something completely different—when a friend passes in the street, an unexpected difficulty is encountered in a line of reasoning, a fire alarm sounds, the desire for a beer suddenly overwhelms the intention to continue writing. Spontaneous though these choices are, they seem not to call for any new general principle of thought . . . they call for much the same principles, only realized in a much more complex total world of desires, goals, and knowledge.

Along similar lines, we might ask whether a computer can ever be emotional. Spock and Bones in *Star Trek* encapsulate two apparently opposite modes of human thought, one with the head and one with the heart. Must a computer problem-solver always be closer to Spock, able only ever to draw the *correct* conclusions from the facts at its disposal?

By now it is probably obvious what I am going to say. How "emotional" the program is made is really up to the programmer. There is nothing in principle to make this especially easy or especially hard. It would be easy to make the program behave exactly the same way on every occasion, drawing just the same inferences from just the same fact . . . but it would also be easy to build in some variability, so that on some days, for example, the program is irritable and more likely to oppose a course of action suggested by another, whereas on other days it is placid and prefers those same choices. It would be easy to build a program to make only specific inferences, based only on knowledge that is certain, or to back much more general hunches. None of these variants would change the general architecture, just the specific ways the architecture is used.

❖

This chapter has discussed how computers can emulate some of the most abstract, powerful, and at first sight mysterious aspects of human thought. Essentially human though it seems to plan a trip to Manchester, the component functions, analyzed through the fifty-year history of artificial intelligence, seem quite comprehensible. There seems no difficulty in principle in making a machine behave in this way: The machine needs just to be filled with the right knowledge and then to reason with this knowledge in the right piecemeal, sequential, humanlike way.

As psychology and neuroscience develop, and in particular as we work with computer models, it seems increasingly likely that, at some point, machines might be built to mimic any kind of human thought and behavior. This may often be difficult in practice—as in the case of computer vision—but seems entirely possible in principle.

At the same time, something inevitably seems to be left out. This is the matter of *experience*. A computer can easily be made to appear irritable on one day and placid on the next; in the future, a computer may reliably distinguish a friend's face in a bustling crowd. But will the computer experience emotion or, for vision, experience one color as red and another as green?

Philosophers of consciousness call the contents of different experiences their *qualia*. In a way that I find slightly disingenuous, they refer to the problem of qualia as "the hard problem." A "hard problem" sounds like a challenge that we know is hard but intend to meet; I would prefer to hear qualia described as "the problem that has us so befuddled that we don't even know what sort of problem it is." What can we possibly imagine saying about a brain event—or an event in any mechanism—that could give it the specific property of a conscious experience, a specific sense of redness or greenness? What paragraph in a research paper or diagram on a whiteboard could explain specifically what it looks like to look red? We have not failed to solve this problem; we have failed even to engage on it.

We know that consciousness is a property of the nervous system. (Other cultures have conceived the possibility that consciousness is found in all objects, in trees or rocks as well as ourselves, but this seems doubtful to me. My own experience is selectively associated with nervous events; I am aware of no separate experience for other objects in my body, such as a liver or fingernail experience.) Furthermore, we know that consciousness is a property of only some nervous events. The earliest stages of the auditory system, for example, decompose sounds into a bank of activity at different frequencies, like a large array of different tuning forks, but nobody can experience an auditory world that is anything like this. About the actual content of experience we know nothing at all: We can say nothing about how nervous events could produce experiences or even about what the experiences themselves are like.

Any child may wonder whether others see red and green in the same way that they see these things themselves. It is impossible to imagine how this question could be answered, and indeed, we rather *assume* that others have experiences like ours than we actually know it. What difference would it make if our friend saw red as we see green, and green as we see red? Indeed, what difference would it make if our friend had no experiences at all but was simply a machine that discriminated these two sensory events and could respond to them with the appropriate verbal labels? For any test we can imagine performing on our friend, it would make no difference at all.

At least for now, I think we have to accept that what I would call not the hard but the impossible problem is just that—not only outside science but beyond all useful conception. By analogy, we may feel it probable that other people have experiences very much like ours, whereas computers, no matter their complexity, do not. I feel this way myself. At the same time, we must accept that this is no more than an analogy. We can pose the question but imagine no possible observation that would bear on the answer. If we are ever to address this question, my suspicion is that it will need some sort of conceptual revolution—a way of thinking that explains what sort of question it is and that so far we have not even imagined.

Like the stickleback courting its mate or the toad hunting a worm, our behavior is built up in complex sequences of simpler parts, sequences that, as they run to completion, achieve a final goal. Unlike the stickleback or toad, however, for the actors in the Cuban plaza, the parts of the behavioral sequence are not the innate releasing mechanisms of much animal behavior. Instead they are the arbitrarily constructed cognitive enclosures of human thought, each assembling just that information that bears on a small, focused subproblem.

As compared to the sequences of other animals, the sequences of human thought are special in several ways. Our human sequences can be arbitrarily long and complex, as we plan moves not just to bring a mate to the nest but to promote goals at the scale of a lifetime or even of a whole culture. The content of our cognitive enclosures can be of any kind, and expressed at any level of abstraction, as we think and set goals in family relations, in sport, in the behavior of financial markets, in the laws of thermodynamics. In our minds, the innate releasing mechanism has been replaced by an almost entirely flexible structure, capable of focus on almost any kind of problem. Wherever we can acquire knowledge, expressed in any form, we can pose problems and set goals in terms of this knowledge. It is assembly of these entirely flexible cognitive enclosures, I suggest, that provides the essentially human element of human intelligence.

We have here a fundamental principle of human thought and behavior. But how does it actually work? How is it constructed in the brain? Now we can return to Luria. Over and over again, as computers use their knowledge to think, we have seen how easy it is to go wrong. Unless just the right knowledge is used in just the right way, the mental program enters the wrong path, goes around in circles, or is completely derailed. The tight structure of goal-directed thought and behavior is loosened. This is just what Luria described in frontal lobe patients.

Some process in the frontal lobe—or, more accurately, in the multiple-demand system examined in chapter 4—must allow useful mental programs to be assembled and run.[15] But what neural process could achieve this? Can it be analyzed? How do frontal neurons actually behave as complex behavior unfolds?

Chapter 6 **Up Close**

I n chapter 4, I described studies of damage to the frontal lobes and the arresting insights they can produce. Neuroscientists often argue that the study of damage is the gold standard for deciding on the functions of a brain area. If a function is changed when an area is damaged, this change shows that the area was in some way essential to that function. The contrast is often made with physiological methods like functional MRI, which measure what the brain *does* as it works. If a particular brain area switches on when we recognize a face, this may not mean that the area was essential for face recognition. It may just be a region whose activity often accompanies face recognition; for example, it might register attention paid to any interesting or attractive object. There is no such uncertainty if damage to this region leaves a patient unable to recognize faces.

Though this argument is sound enough, it is also limited. With complex systems, the best question may not always be which part of the system is essential for which part of its activity. Many aspects of system activity result from different parts acting together. Though we may not find this obvious for a system like the brain, something far from clearly understood, it is extremely obvious for systems we understand well.

Here is an example. About ten years ago, my mother-in-law was admitted to the hospital because she was short of breath. Investigation showed that the root cause was a hardened heart valve. It is logically correct to say that a flexible heart valve is essential to prevent shortness of breath, but it is not an especially useful thing to say. To understand the function of the heart valve, it would not be especially profitable to damage it and then measure shortness of breath. Rather more profitable are likely to be physiological measurements of the movement of the valve and their correlation with the heartbeat.

A range of methods can be used to make physiological measurements of brain activity. In functional MRI, activity might be measured in a three-millimeter cube of brain, around the size of a small peppercorn. Small though it is, this cube might contain several million brain cells or neurons with different properties and functions. Of course, combining activity across so many cells brings limits on the information we can obtain. Imagine that an observer from outer space was trying to understand the principles of human conversation. Functional MRI would be like taking average measurements of the volume of speech from whole cities. The method could doubtless show some facts about the way people communicate. It would show that peaks and troughs of conversational output occur on a twenty-four-hour cycle. It might reveal eruptions of noise around critical sporting events. In the brain we are luckier, because the neurons in one region have similar interests, as though one city discussed politics and another philosophy. Just the same, it is obvious that, like the observer from outer space, what we really need is to listen to the detailed speech of individual people. In the brain this means recording the exact messages received and transmitted by individual neurons. This method is known as single cell neurophysiology. It gives us the best, most detailed window we have onto what brains do as they work.

In chapter 3, I described how all brain function is a matter of many million brain cells or neurons, combining and transmitting information in a complex web of activity. In the optic tectum of the toad, for example, a neuron combines inputs from different "patch detectors" in the eye to indicate the presence of a long, thin, wormlike object moving in the correct direction to be a worm. This message is then sent on toward motor (movement-related) regions that will control approaching and snapping. In the visual system of monkeys and other mammals, including ourselves, regions in the occipital lobe form maps of the visual image that is projected onto the eye. In such a map, for example, a particular cell might code the presence of a line crossing one small part of the image; by combining information from many such cells, further cells downstream might build up the description of a particular object with a particular shape, such as a face or cup. Following the early maps, further brain areas extract many different properties of the visual world: shapes, colors, textures, movements, and so on. In different parts of the brain, neurons code many other kinds of information: sounds, smells, memories, movements.

In all these cases, information is "coded" by the rate of firing brief electrical impulses or spikes. In the simplest case, we might speak as if a neuron were "on" or "off," firing spikes when its conditions are satisfied (the worm is present, a particular tone is heard) and otherwise remaining silent. More realistically, we imagine that any change in firing rate transmits information to other cells. A worm detector, for example, might fire extremely strongly when the perfect worm enters the field of view, less strongly for an object that somewhat resembles a worm, and not at all for a looming human. Indeed, since most cells have some baseline or spontaneous firing rate, this rate can even decrease in the presence of a highly inappropriate input, showing active inhibition of this cell's activity. The principle is shown in figure 8, with the activity of an imaginary worm detector cell. Before

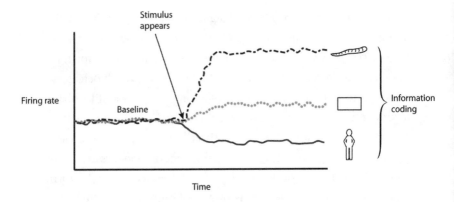

Figure 8. Firing rates of an imaginary worm detector neuron, before (left) and after (right) one of three stimuli appears.

any stimulus appears (left part of figure), the cell fires at some spontaneous or baseline rate. Small, moment-by-moment fluctuations in this rate reflect the noise or variability seen in all neurons. Then when a stimulus appears (center), the rate of firing suddenly changes. For a worm, there is a large increase. For a rectangle, the increase is smaller. For a person, there is active inhibition. These three different firing rates potentially inform cells in the rest of the toad's brain what stimulus has appeared. In response to these different firing rates, for example, motor cells might choose either to approach or to freeze.

With a tiny electrode inserted into the brain, spikes can be recorded from single neurons, like a detailed record of a single person's speech. Occasionally, recordings of this sort can be made in humans, usually when electrodes are placed in the brain to gather critical information for neurosurgery. The electrodes do not hurt, just as brain surgery itself does not hurt, and can perfectly well be carried out in a patient who is awake, because unlike the skin and other organs, the brain has no sensory receptors and feels nothing. For a few days before the surgery, an electrode sits in the patient's brain and can be used to ask what is happening in a small number of neurons surrounding its tip. Recordings made while the subject carries out some controlled activity, perhaps speaking a sentence or retrieving a memory, can give one small link between neural activity and behavior. For systematic experiments, however, it is important to place electrodes exactly, targeting just the right brain structure; to sample neurons widely within that structure; and to gather data over many sessions of recording under tightly controlled circumstances. For experiments of this sort, accordingly, almost all of our information comes from recordings made in awake, behaving animals.

Since the nineteenth century, neurophysiology has been dominated by a central thought. The firing of any one cell has a specific meaning, and by careful experimentation with different stimuli and conditions, the physiologist can discover what that meaning is. Firing in one cell indicates a worm; in another, a flash of red; in another, pain; in another, a command to raise the hand or move the eyes to the left. Explicitly or implicitly, and to a greater or lesser degree, this idea has guided our conceptualizations of brain function, the design of physiological experiments, and the interpretation of their results. In 1826, Johannes Müller called it the law of specific nerve energies.[1]

With groundbreaking studies in the early 1970s, single cell recording came late to the frontal lobes. (An exception is the motor or movement-related cortex in the posterior part of the frontal lobes. In this chapter I am talking about the more anterior parts, generally called the prefrontal cortex.) The story of this work is fascinating, documenting the attempt and failure to find the specific nerve energies of frontal cells. Instead of fixed meanings for the firing of each cell, the activity of frontal cells shows massive flexibility and adaptation to context. The experiments detail the creation of a cognitive enclosure and the shift from one enclosure to the next as a mental program unfolds.

There is a good reason why single cell neurophysiology began not in the complex world of the frontal lobes but in simpler sensory and motor systems. The search for the specific meaning of a cell's firing—for the exact conditions that determine its activity—is at best a long, sometimes fruitless activity. Even early in the visual system, for example, where it is certain that the world one should explore is the world of visual stimulation, it was a tour de force to discover what stimuli are needed to understand neuronal activity—for example, that the best stimulus to drive activity in one cell might be a bright central bar oriented forty-five degrees to the vertical, enclosed in a dark surround, all placed in one very precise part of the visual image projected onto the eye. In a more complex system, the problem is even more unconstrained. If one has isolated a frontal lobe cell for recording, what properties of sensory stimulation or motor output or the animal's state or the task performed should be investigated as possible clues to this cell's function?

The clue that neurophysiologists first decided to pursue came from a classic experiment on the effect of frontal lobe removals in the monkey. In this experiment, reported by Carlyle Jacobsen in 1935, monkeys had to solve an apparently simple test of short-term memory.[2] They watched a piece of food being hidden in one of two alternative locations; waited a few seconds; and then had to reach out to the correct location to obtain the food they had seen hidden. After surgical removal of the prefrontal cortex, these animals showed severe difficulties in completing the task. The result suggested that short-term memory could be a key aspect of frontal lobe function.

Thirty-six years later, two neurophysiologists, Joaquín Fuster and Garrett Alexander, took up the story.[3] Single cell recording experiments in awake monkeys were just beginning to show their potential in analysis of the motor system. In these experiments, monkeys were trained to carry out many trials of an experimental task; recording in the primary motor cortex, neurophysiologists had begun to ask how these neurons created commands for movement.[4] With these successful experiments as their lead, Fuster and Alexander decided to study short-term memory in the frontal lobe. They adapted Jacobsen's experiment for neurophysiology. On each trial, the monkey watched as food was hidden in one of two containers. There was a delay, then the monkey was allowed to reach out to the container where he remembered the food had been hidden. Adventuring into a new world, Fuster and Alexander lowered microelectrodes into the prefrontal cortex, found single neurons, and recorded their spikes as the animal carried out his task.

The results were spectacular. Just as they had predicted, Fuster and Alexander found themselves surrounded by short-term memory cells. Time after time, they encountered neurons that behaved as short-term memory cells should, beginning to fire when the stimulus was hidden at the start of the trial, sustaining this firing throughout the following delay, and then abruptly terminating as the monkey was allowed to reach out and gather the reward. Critically, cells coded the *contents* of short-term memory; very often, their firing in the delay period was at two different rates, *depending on whether the reward location was to the right or the left*. In other words, the firing of these cells could be taken as a sustained signal of where the monkey should reach at the end of the trial—a sustained signal of what location the monkey was currently holding in mind.

With this experiment, it seemed that the adventure of frontal lobe neurophysiology was already an extraordinary success. Based on a lead from just one previous idea of frontal lobe function, physiological recordings had provided an immediate, spectacular window into what frontal neurons do. Already the results suggested a specific function, or a kind of specific nerve energy—a role in preserving information in an animal's short-term memory.

Over the following twenty years, a succession of quite beautiful experiments refined these conclusions. Following Jacobsen's first experiment, more detailed studies had shown that short-term memory is especially impaired by lesions in one particular region of the prefrontal cortex—a fold in the lateral surface known as the principal sulcus. Attention accordingly focused on neurons in this specific region and their activity in a variety of more sophisticated versions of Jacobsen's experiment. It is worth stopping to note that, with time and patience, monkeys can learn many complex tasks, with all kinds of stimuli, responses, decisions, and rewards such as juice or fruit. Once the task has been learned, neurophysiological experiments can ask how neurons behave as this task is carried out.

For the next generation of short-term memory experiments, Shintaro Funahashi, Charles Bruce, and Patricia Goldman-Rakic turned to a new task.[5] On each trial, the task began with a light flashed in one of eight possible positions around a circle. The animal held his eyes still at the center of the circle through the short-term memory delay, and then, when a signal showed that the delay was over, he made an immediate eye movement to the place where the original light had flashed. If this movement was correct, he was rewarded with a drop of juice. Though now there was no hidden food, again the task required short-term memory for a specific stimulus position.

With eight stimulus positions, the experimenters were able to plot short-term memory activity with exquisite precision. As they had hoped, many cells in the principal sulcus coded specific stimulus locations. One cell, for example, might fire most strongly during memory of the top left location, with weaker firing for the two locations to either side of this best one, and little firing at all elsewhere. Others would have strongest firing for other positions. Put together, the pattern of firing across the whole cell population showed exactly which position the animal was holding in mind. Within the principal sulcus, the experiment showed a neural code quite sufficient for short-term memory—sufficient to hold the correct location in mind across the memory delay and then to direct the eye movement that would produce a reward.

Further experiments pursued a related question. At the back of the brain, the analysis of visual information proceeds along two somewhat parallel routes.[6] (Again a look at fig. 3 in chapter 3 may help.) One route, leading from the occipital into the temporal lobe, is concerned with *what* objects are present in the visual scene—with object recognition. Often this is called the ventral stream (ventral meaning toward the bottom of the brain). A second, leading from the occipital to the parietal lobe, is concerned more with *where* objects are, in particular for the control of spatially directed behavior, such as reaching and grasping. Often this is called the dorsal stream (dorsal meaning toward the top of the brain). The idea arose that something similar might be true for short-term memory activity in the prefrontal cortex. Perhaps more dorsal parts of the prefrontal cortex—including the principal sulcus—would underlie short-term memory for locations, as in the Jacobsen task and its descendants, whereas more ventral regions—more directly connected to the temporal lobes—would handle short-term memory for object identities. Figure 9 shows a lateral (side) view of the monkey's brain, with dorsal and ventral regions marked on the frontal lobe. Experiments began searching for object-related activity—for example, short-term memory for faces—in ventral regions. Again, the results were as predicted.[7]

With hindsight, perhaps, this may have been the moment to begin suspecting that everything was going too well. After all, Jacobsen's

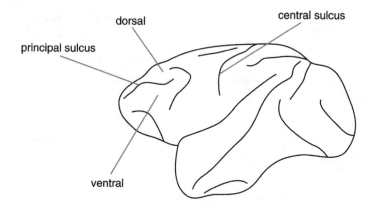

Figure 9. Lateral view of the monkey brain showing dorsal and ventral regions of the frontal lobe.

experiment on short-term memory was just one of many windows into the complex effects of frontal lobe lesions. What of Luria? What of Bianchi and his monkeys who seemed to lack purposeful, structured behavior? What of the surgeon Penfield and his sister? Could all of the complex disorganization of frontal lobe patients be explained by a loss of short-term memory and by separate memory modules in discrete parts of the frontal lobe? Many scientists wondered about this question. Fuster himself, certainly, thought that his short-term memory activity had to be just one small part of the frontal lobe puzzle.[8] Still, the exquisite neurophysiological results seemed so compelling. Recording the activity of single microscopic neurons, one could see actual short-term memory at work.

The picture finally began to unravel with a critical experiment reported in 1997 by Chenchal Rao, Gregor Rainer, and Earl Miller.[9] The leader of the laboratory, Earl Miller, is a good friend of mine; we had carried out single cell recordings together in 1989–1990, when I had visited the laboratory of Robert Desimone at the National Institute of Mental Health, outside Washington, D.C. Our experiments with Desimone had concerned a topic that returns later in the chapter (the neurophysiology of selective attention in the visual system). Now Miller had moved to the Massachusetts Institute of Technology and was setting up his own neurophysiology laboratory. This was one of his first experiments.

For a variety of reasons, Miller had come to doubt the clean separation between "what" and "where" memory in the prefrontal cortex—between memory for objects and locations. Accordingly, the group set up a new experiment in which the activity of the same neuron could be recorded both for memory of what and, later in the same trial, for memory of where. They made their recordings from a large area on the lateral surface of the frontal cortex, including both dorsal and ventral parts.

The task went like this (fig. 10). Each trial began with a single dot in the middle of a computer screen. The dot waited until the monkey moved his eyes to look straight toward it (labeled "Fixation" in fig. 10), then as soon as the monkey was watching the right place, the dot was replaced by a picture, also shown at the center of the screen. This picture was an instruction. It told the monkey what his target object would be for this trial.

After the target picture turned off, there was a first short delay. This was the "what" delay. During this delay, all that the monkey had to do was remember the identity of the target while continuing to hold his eyes steady in the center.

Next came a second picture display. This time there were two different pictures, placed in different possible positions (above, below, to the left, or to the right of screen center; in fig. 10 the pictures are shown above and to the left). Just one of the pictures matched the original target. The monkey still had to keep his eyes in the middle,

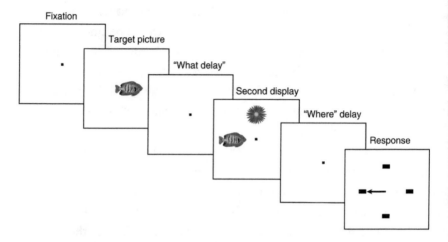

Figure 10. The series of events (moving from left to right) for one trial of the task used by Rao, Rainer, and Miller. Each panel shows a view of the computer screen as seen by the monkey. The arrow on the final screen shows the correct response.

but now when the two pictures disappeared, he had to remember where the target had been. Following another delay (the "where" delay), he was finally cued to respond. The cue was a display of four dots, showing where pictures might have appeared in the second display. Now the monkey was rewarded with juice if he made an eye movement to the correct position: the place where he remembered that the target picture had been seen in the second picture display. In fig. 10 the correct movement is shown with an arrow, but in the experiment, obviously, there was no arrow on the screen. To choose his response and finally obtain the reward, the monkey had to remember the correct position.

The beauty of the experiment is in the change of direction that is required midtrial. During the first delay, the animal remembers the identity of the target. During the second delay, this no longer matters;

all the monkey must know now is where the target appeared, which is where he must finally look to obtain the juice.

The task changes direction, and at the same moment, frontal neurons changed direction, too. During the first delay, many cells coded target identity, just as they had coded object identity in previous recordings from the ventral prefrontal cortex. As usual, this code came in the form of different firing rates for different possible target objects. But in the second delay, many of these same cells now coded target location. Now they behaved in the same way as the cells previously recorded in the principal sulcus.

There were not two separate sets of cells at all. Though cells were recorded from both ventral and dorsal regions, results from the two were the same. Instead of two separate sets of cells, there were two separate parts of the task. What frontal neurons did was to do as they were told. They did whatever was needed.

Events moved rapidly after this first experiment. Again, many of the critical experiments came from the Miller laboratory. They showed that indeed:[10]

Things had been going too well in the short-term memory experiments. It was true that, if the task required short-term memory, many frontal neurons would show beautiful short-term memory activity. But if the task required something different, then it would be this something different that frontal neurons did. As in the Rao, Rainer, and Miller experiments, frontal neurons did what they were told.

Even within one task, frontal neurons might do many different things. Some, if the task required it, might code the contents of short-term memory. Some might code the identity of task stimuli or, like a command to move, might fire at the time of the monkey's response. Some might code the rule that was in force—for example, to move the eyes toward or away from a flashing light. Some might code what reward the animal was currently working for, perhaps juice versus cabbage. Very often, as in the Rao, Rainer, and Miller study, the same neuron would do several things at once.

For frontal cells, there was no specific nerve energy. Each cell's firing had no fixed meaning. Instead, its meaning held *only in the context of the current task*. When the context changed, then the cell's activity changed, too.

Recordings in several regions of prefrontal cortex gave surprisingly similar results. Whatever the region and whatever the task, the astonishing result was just how many frontal neurons coded the specific events of this task. This was why the experiments always worked so well. It did not really matter what task the animal was trained to do or where the recordings were made. Whatever the task and recording area, the experiment always showed exquisite patterns of task-related activity.

In the short-term memory experiments, recordings had been made in just one, carefully crafted experimental task. They had been made in specific, carefully chosen regions of prefrontal cortex. When exactly the right pattern of activity was found in exactly the right place, it seemed that the experimenters' hypothesis had been dramatically confirmed. The new data showed what an extraordinary trap this had been. All the care that had gone into the design of these experiments had been unnecessary. Almost any task and (within a large area of prefrontal cortex) almost any recording location would have done just as well. What frontal neurons did was tell us what we wanted to hear.

This picture unfolded in a series of experiments requiring monkeys to carry out tasks of ever greater diversity and complexity. The picture was always the same. The animal learned to carry out the task. The experimenter recorded activity from randomly selected prefrontal neurons. Though cells were arbitrarily selected from among uncounted millions that could have been recorded, maybe 50 percent of those examined—sometimes more, sometimes less—did just what the experimenter was looking for. They coded the exact information and events of this particular experiment.

Let me illustrate with two more experiments from the Miller laboratory. In the first of these, monkeys were trained to discriminate cats from dogs.[11] The set of stimuli was based around three prototype "cats" (different species from the cat family) and three prototype "dogs," but the clever feature of the experiment was the use of morphing software to create stimuli that were some compromise between one prototype and another, either a compromise between two prototypes of the same category or a compromise between a cat and a dog. In some cases, this created stimuli that were cats but quite doglike (a morph that was 60 percent of a cat but 40 percent of a dog) or dogs that were quite catlike (the reverse proportions). On each trial, the monkey saw two of these stimuli in turn. His task was to decide if they both came from the same category, making one response for either two cats or two dogs but a different response for one of each. The complex set of stimuli was accordingly to be sorted into just two categories: even a 60 percent cat being considered "cat," and even a 60 percent dog being considered "dog."

The task required complex object categorization, and in about 20 percent of randomly selected prefrontal cells, complex object categorization is what was seen. Cells would respond in one way to cats and a different way to dogs—whether cats and dogs were pure prototypes or morphs that were hard to categorize. For example, a morph that was 60 percent cat and 40 percent dog was in physical terms closely similar to a morph that was 40 percent cat and 60 percent dog—but the cells, like the task, treated these two differently.

What sense can these results make? Obviously it is not true that, among the many millions of cells of prefrontal cortex, about 20 percent are cat or dog detectors. The only reasonable conclusion is that, in the context of this task, the cells have become cat and dog detectors. They are making the discrimination that the animal is making. They are making the discrimination that is required.

A second experiment of this sort showed how frontal neurons can count.[12] This time, the animal saw displays containing varying numbers of dots. On each trial, as before, two displays were presented in turn, and the animal was to decide whether they were "same" or "different." Specifically, his task was to decide whether the two displays contained the same number of dots, ignoring irrelevant variations in such other display features as dot size or density. The experiment required counting, and now frontal cells counted. As in the short-term memory experiments, they did so with exquisite precision: one cell, for example, might respond best to one specific number, less well to adjacent numbers, and little if at all to numbers farther away. Again it makes no sense to suppose that, among the many millions of cells of the frontal lobe, a good proportion are number detectors. They have become number detectors because the task requires number discrimination.

Experiments could be continued in this vein, but perhaps there is no more point. In experiments of this sort, we now know what we will find. We will find whatever it is we are looking for.

In the previous chapter we considered thought as a sequence of cognitive enclosures. In each enclosure, a small amount of information is assembled to solve one small subproblem. Subproblems can have any content, each calling on a different combination of facts to guide a specific step of thought or action. To create these cognitive enclosures, we need activity in the brain that can be programmed. Like a conventional digital computer, we need a process to assemble just those facts and actions that each new step of the program requires.

Now, in the activity of prefrontal neurons, we have found something very like this. Across the recording area examined in these experiments there are many millions of cells. For each new task, however, we find that enormous numbers of these cells—sometimes, almost all of them—code some kind of information that bears on this task. Sometimes the information is rather general; a neuron may fire, for example, at the time a trial starts or when a reward is delivered. Sometimes the information is very specific, like the selective response to cats versus dogs. Together, however, many millions of cells are configured to code just those objects and events that this particular task involves. The system is filled with the specific information that this particular task requires.

When these experiments started, nobody expected anything like this. By analogy with simple sensory and motor systems, the expectation was for dedicated neurons like worm or edge detectors. For the creation of mental programs, however, dedicated neurons are not the brain's solution.

Of course, these single cell results are very much consistent with "multiple-demand" activity in functional MRI. Looking back at figure 6 in chapter 4, you see the common pattern of brain activity produced by many different cognitive demands: by subtle sensory discriminations, counterintuitive response choices, retrieval of words from a memorized list, solution of novel puzzles, and many more. A programmable system should indeed show multiple-demand activity. Its neurons will be active in many varied tasks, in solution of many different problems.

As shown in figure 6, the brain has several multiple-demand regions. There is a large area of activity toward the back of the lateral frontal surface; a second on the upper part of the medial surface; a third in the parietal lobe. Exact correspondences are not known between human and monkey brains; in the monkey experiments, however, the great majority of frontal recordings have been made toward the rear of the lateral surface, and it is reasonable to suppose that, roughly at least, this corresponds to the large lateral multiple-demand region in human functional MRI.

What of neurons in other parts of the multiple-demand system? At this stage, we know relatively little, though some experiments have suggested properties resembling those of the lateral prefrontal cells, with flexible, task-relevant responses of many kinds.[13] From human functional MRI we would infer an integrated system whose parts almost always work together. Only for one part of this system, however, do we have much detailed information on what its neurons *do*—on the detailed conversation of individuals.

A cognitive enclosure requires *attention*: a focus on just those few facts or considerations that bear on the current problem. Many kinds of experiments have studied the properties of attention, from experiments in human behavior to experiments in neurophysiology. Though attention has many sides, the most popular problem for experimental investigation has been attention in perception, or awareness of some sensory inputs at the expense of others.

I described classical auditory examples in chapter 1, with experiments on simultaneous speech messages. After a minute of listening carefully to a man speaking from the left, a person knows almost nothing of what a woman said on the right—not what the woman's message was about, not what language it was in, not whether it was played backwards. The same thing applies to visual events. For example, two video sequences are played at once on the same screen, so that they completely overlap.[14] One shows two pairs of hands playing a slapping game; the other shows men playing basketball; the subject is told to spend a minute or so watching the basketball. In the middle of the hand game, the players stop, solemnly shake hands, then proceed.

At the end of the minute, the subject is asked if anything strange happened in the slapping game. His eyes were right on the game for the full minute, but the handshake often came and went unseen.

Many single cell experiments have also examined attention in the monkey. The most commonly studied problem has been visual attention, as in the handshake example—in the monkey's visual system, what separates the object that is attended from the object that is ignored? The results provide a nice complement to what we have seen in frontal lobe cells.

A highly influential example comes from the work of Jeffrey Moran and Robert Desimone, published in 1985.[15] In human vision, you might say that attention filters the sensory input: some things are allowed in, while much else is kept out. In the Moran and Desimone experiment, this same filtering was shown in single cells of the monkey visual system.

Earlier I described the successive analysis of visual objects along the ventral processing stream that runs from the occipital to the temporal lobes. Though Moran and Desimone recorded at several locations along this stream, we can concentrate on one region in the occipital lobe, an area called V4. Like cells in earlier parts of the visual system, V4 cells have a restricted "receptive field," responding just to stimuli in one small part of the visual image. For example, if the eye is directed to the center of a computer screen, a V4 cell might respond just to a smallish patch on the upper left. Within its receptive field, a typical V4 cell will respond well to bars with a certain combination of length, orientation, color, and possibly other features, such as a short red bar tilted left. This "good" stimulus produces strong activity when it appears in the receptive field; for another stimulus, such as a long yellow bar tilted right, there is less activity or even none at all. Like the worm detectors in the toad, this V4 cell is a short red left-tilted detector.

The Moran and Desimone experiment worked like this. Each visual display contained two stimuli. One was the good stimulus for this cell; the other was chosen to be a poor stimulus. The two stimuli were placed at different locations, A and B, both within the cell's receptive field. Before the trial began, the monkey received a cue telling him whether he should pay attention to location A or B. (As usual in these experiments, the monkey always kept his gaze fixed on the center of the screen while paying attention to the off-center location A or B. In this way, the visual image on the eye remained constant through the trial.) The stimulus at the cued location was relevant to the task; the other, like the handshake, could be ignored.

When the good stimulus appeared at the cued location, the cell responded strongly. This is what we should expect: the short-red-left detector was shown a short-red-left bar, and it responded. When the same stimulus appeared but the animal moved its attention to the other location, the response of the cell was cut off. Just as we filter out the handshake, the V4 cell filtered out the good—but unattended—bar.

We now know more of what the cell does when the good bar is unattended. At least to a first approximation, what it does is to fire as though it were looking just at the other, poor bar.[16] This of course is the bar that is receiving the animal's attention. The V4 cell responds to the attended bar and filters out the other.

You may certainly say that the V4 cell has a dedicated function, or a specific nerve energy. In a very dedicated way, it detects short-red-left bars. But you may also say that it has some flexibility, or sensitivity to context. If two different stimuli are present in the receptive field, both have the potential to drive activity in the cell. But the one that actually drives activity is the one that is attended, or fits into the current cognitive enclosure.

Now it can be seen that frontal cells do something similar, but more so. For a V4 cell, inputs come just from one small part of the visual field. Still, the cell has the flexibility to respond to one of these inputs or another, depending on its relevance to the current task. In frontal cells, there is a kind of super-attention. Many different inputs, from many systems in the brain, converge onto the prefrontal cortex. Within the prefrontal cortex, information is passed widely from one cell to another. For any one cell, accordingly, there is potential access to many kinds of information. Apparently what cells do is adapt to code just that information that belongs in the current task—just those things, whatever they are, that belong in the current focus of attention.

Though I have spoken of prefrontal cells as creating cognitive enclosures, all parts of the brain work by interaction with others. Following Moran and Desimone, many subsequent experiments have shown how attention controls activity in many parts of the brain. In visual, auditory, and other sensory systems, in occipital, parietal, temporal, and frontal lobes, attended stimuli produce strong responses, whereas unattended stimuli are lost. The strength of this filtering varies from one brain region to another and from one task to another, but in very many systems and very many tasks, some degree of filtering is the rule. In a sense, all these systems are converging to work on the content of the current enclosure.

This conclusion brings up a point mentioned in chapter 3. Although the brain is to some degree modular, with dedicated components performing dedicated functions, equally important is the question of integration. Typically we do not look at one thing, listen to another, and think about a third. We perform an integrated, coherent activity or task, combining many sorts of processing in service of a common goal.

Again, visual attention has been a good test bed for the study of integration. One object in the visual field—for example, a cat approaching from the left—has many properties. It has a certain shape and color, a certain direction of travel, a certain current location with respect to the hand that reaches out to stroke it. To a degree at least, these different properties are coded in different parts of the visual system. When we attend to the cat, however, what we see is the whole cat, with its shape, color, motion, and location. Behavioral experiments confirm that this is really the case, and experiments in functional MRI show how, when attention is directed to an object, activity changes in the many separate visual areas that code different properties of that object. The conclusion must be that activity is integrated across the different parts of the brain's visual system. The system avoids incoherent activity; it attends to all those features that belong together as parts of the same thing.[17]

Integration probably happens in many ways, some quite local, such as integrating the different properties of one visual object, and others operating over a wider range of mental contents. With their broad connections, prefrontal cells may be critical in wide-scale integration. The prefrontal cortex is special not only in the breadth of its inputs but also in the breadth of its outputs to other parts of the brain. The thought would be that, as a cognitive enclosure is established, just the information that belongs in this enclosure is coded in the prefrontal cortex. At the same time, many other parts of the brain follow suit, to the degree that they are able—visual cells coding relevant visual events, auditory cells coding relevant sounds, other parts of the brain delivering relevant facts from long-term memory or relevant motivations and desires. Through the broad connections of the prefrontal cortex—and possibly, other multiple-demand regions—the whole body of work is integrated. The cognitive enclosure is assembled; the mental program is kept on track.

In any real mental program, distinct cognitive enclosures follow one another in rapid succession. For a second, we search in our pocket for the car keys; next we are moving into the car seat; a few seconds later we are checking for traffic as we pull out into the street. If prefrontal cells control mental programs, they must make these same, high-speed transitions from one cognitive enclosure to the next, abandoning the last as it is completed and moving at once to the next.

Already we can see a transition of this sort in the what-where experiment of Rao, Rainer, and Miller. In the first delay, the critical fact was the identity of the target. This was the information that the monkey needed to retain for later in the trial; in the prefrontal cortex, many neurons held onto this information. After the second display, target identity was no longer important. Whatever the target had been, now the critical fact was only where it had been presented. Now, many neurons coded target position, and at the same time, their previous code of target identity was lost.

Though this question of transition between enclosures is critical, experiments are only just beginning to address it directly. I can illustrate with some of my own studies of the behavior of prefrontal cells, carried out in Oxford with a long-term friend and guide, David Gaffan. This is demanding work, as we search for order in the complex, ever-changing activity patterns of prefrontal neurons. Already, though, we can see hints of a fascinating picture beginning to emerge.

Think back to the experiment on cats and dogs. To run an experiment of this sort, monkeys may be trained for a year or more before the task is fully learned. As you might imagine, the task is built up in stages, so that the monkey learns the many facts he needs to control his mental program: that he should pay attention to the pictures on the screen; that juice comes from a drinking spout; that he is rewarded for a particular kind of movement; that the movement should depend on the pictures. In particular, the monkey will be trained for months on the specific visual categories that the task involves: that all pictures more than 50 percent cat belong in the category of "cats," whereas all pictures more than 50 percent dog belong in the category "dogs." The experiment shows many "cat" and "dog" detectors in the prefrontal cortex, but why? We should like to conclude that these detectors reflect the current cognitive enclosure—the decision that the monkey is making right at this second. There is, however, an alternative possibility, also interesting but quite different. Could it be that these cat and dog detectors have been permanently created by the long training that the monkey has received, so that even if the immediate task changed, the detectors would remain?

In the cat-dog task, there is already some evidence that the immediate task does matter;[18] and here is another set of experiments addressing the same sort of question. In our studies, monkeys watch a stream of pictures waiting for a particular target. When the target appears, the monkey makes an eye movement to receive a reward; for nontarget pictures, he holds his eyes still and continues to watch. Two versions of the task are used.[19]

In the first version, the same picture is the target through months of training. In the prefrontal cortex, we find that many cells behave as target detectors, responding strongly to the target but little if at all to nontargets. This is the familiar story again: in this task, it is targets that matter, and it is targets that frontal neurons detect.

Now we use a second version. This time, each picture in the experiment is a target on some trials but a nontarget on others. A cue at the start of the trial instructs the monkey which picture to look for. Now the logic of the task—the way that the cognitive enclosure should be constructed—varies from one trial to the next. Again, though, prefrontal cells follow suit. On one trial, a cell responds strongly to the target; on the next trial, this same cell ignores this same picture, which is now a nontarget. Almost unbelievably, prefrontal cells have been reprogrammed trial by trial, responding in line with the specific, current, momentary cognitive enclosure.

We can go on to ask about transitions, not from one trial to the next, but between events within one trial. In the second version of the task—the one with an instruction cue at the beginning of each trial—the monkey needs to know what this instruction was. The instruction cue sets up the enclosure for this trial—it tells the animal which picture to look for. Immediately after the cue is presented, while the animal waits for the picture series to begin, up to 30 percent of all cells code cue identity. They fire at different rates depending on which cue was presented. I still find it incredible that this happens— that almost a third of *all cells we can record* produce different activity as the animal prepares a search for different possible targets. Across the prefrontal cortex, vast numbers of cells are configured to help in this one small task. Less than a second later, once the picture stream has begun, most of this activity has gone. Apparently, it is needed just to establish the correct decision rule, not later to maintain it.

There is a last intriguing result from this experiment. In this same version of the task, there are really several subtasks to perform on each trial, each with different content and mental operations. When the instruction cue is presented, the animal must use it to query long-term memory, bringing the correct target to mind. (The instruction cues are also pictures, with a different instruction picture paired to each possible target.) In the delay between one picture and the next, the animal must wait, hold his eyes still, and continue to hold the correct target in mind. As each subsequent picture is presented, the animal must classify this new visual input as target or nontarget and prepare or withhold an eye movement. Once again, there is a series of steps in a mental program, just like any program you might write for your computer.

Now we can look at a whole group of prefrontal cells and ask how the whole pattern of activity changes from one step of the program to the next.[20] The answer is that these patterns are almost completely independent. In each pattern, many neurons are firing relatively strongly, while many others are relatively silent. Any one neuron may fire strongly in one step of the program, or two, or three . . . its activity in any one step tells us nothing of what it will do in another. Mathematically, the patterns are uncorrelated.

What does this mean? As the mental program moves from step to step, so there are corresponding transitions from one state of prefrontal activity to another. Each state is presumably important in assembling just the right set of cognitive operations—coding the information that these operations require and supporting related activity in many different systems of the brain. Uncorrelated patterns have advantages because they are easy to tell apart. Even if the system has error or noise, so that some neurons fire at the wrong rate, it is very hard to confuse one uncorrelated pattern with another. The ability of the prefrontal cortex to produce these patterns may be essential in keeping the separate steps of a mental program clearly intact and distinct. In prefrontal cells, again, the mental program is kept on track.

If a cell has a specific nerve energy, it is obvious how its signal could be used. A worm detector signals the presence of a worm and can be used to direct an approach and snap. This is much less obvious for a neuron whose function is not dedicated, so that the same rate of firing may mean target detection at one moment and then something completely different, perhaps delivery of reward, a moment later. Can a signal of this sort ever be effectively used?

To address this question, we need formal computer models based on artificial neurons and their connections. Can a signal like the one we see in prefrontal cells be used for effective control of the system? Again, it is early days for this work, but some promising results are beginning to appear.[21] If any one prefrontal cell is randomly connected to large numbers of other, more dedicated cells elsewhere in the brain, then indeed, activity in this one prefrontal cell can help create and stabilize many different kinds of cognitive enclosures. With feedback from one cell to another, the model's artificial cells can look very much like real prefrontal cells, active in many different mental activities and coding many different kinds of momentarily task-relevant information. Models of this sort may be off track, and certainly they miss much of the complexity and richness of real neurons and brains. Still, they show that a highly flexible, context-specific neural signal is usable in principle.

The neurophysiological data tell a story of highly flexible function in prefrontal cells. As each new cognitive problem is posed, the neurons of the prefrontal cortex adapt their behavior to solve it—like the many cells that become cat or dog detectors or, in a different task, count the number of dots. Perhaps this flexibility can help to explain some of the puzzles left open at the end of chapter 4.

One question comes from functional MRI data, and the spread of prefrontal activity as a task becomes more demanding. Although increased demand strengthens activity in multiple-demand regions, sometimes there is also a spread forward into more anterior parts of the frontal lobe. Does this reflect new functions or more neurons involved in the same function? If the system is inherently flexible, an increasing spread of activity may be the natural expectation as task demands increase. It could make sense, for example, for cells to be brought into play until the different components of the task are adequately organized; with more components, more cells may be needed and activity may be seen to spread. Though this is a speculation, it is an idea that fits well with the characteristic adaptability of frontal responses. New single cell recording experiments would be needed to test it.

The same sort of idea may help to explain the sense of fuzzy double dissociations that I described for human and monkey lesions.

In a clear double dissociation, a lesion to one part of the frontal lobe would impair one cognitive function X, whereas a lesion to a different part would impair a different function Y. In the case of frontal lesions, however, we have a repeated sense of double dissociations that are almost real, but not quite. One lesion may be most harmful to function X, another to function Y, but all the time, there is a background sense that, to some degree at least, most lesions impair most functions.

Again, this could make sense in a system that is characteristically flexible. It is unlikely that, across the prefrontal cortex, cells in all regions are equally suited to all functions. Some of the evidence that I discussed in chapter 4 tells strongly against this, especially as we move outside the multiple-demand regions. In any case, different parts of the prefrontal cortex have different connections to the rest of the brain, determining the information they most directly receive. Still, information is liberally exchanged between different frontal regions, and very likely, a cell that does not receive information directly can receive it by some roundabout route. Under the right circumstances, it may adapt for many different functions. Though their roles may not all be equal, cells in many regions may contribute to solution of the same cognitive problems.

An inherent flexibility, finally, could help to explain the astonishing resistance that we sometimes see to frontal lobe damage. In two different patients, much the same lesion produces radically different effects: while one patient is severely impaired, the other seems essentially unchanged, returning to work and to normal life. A system that is characteristically flexible may have a natural defense against damage. When the "best" cells for some operation are damaged, the system may respond by drafting others into service. In some patients, this seems to work almost perfectly, and large amounts of tissue are lost with little apparent effect. Of course, we have no clue why this should be possible for one person and apparently impossible for another. What are the detailed mechanisms and limits of such functional reorganization? At present, we have no idea.

It is time to come back to the story. In chapter 4 I described frontal lobe patients and their deficits in the active control of behavior—in structuring, organizing, and running an effective mental program. In chapter 5 we considered what it takes to construct such a program, with successive cognitive enclosures working on segmented, focused subproblems. Now the single cell data show how neurons of the prefrontal cortex have just the properties needed to construct a mental program, moving flexibly and rapidly from one focused cognitive enclosure to the next.

Construction of a cognitive enclosure requires focus on what matters—on the facts, rules, and operations that belong in this small subproblem. The single cell data show how prefrontal neurons define the separate stages of a task, emphasizing just that information that matters in this stage. The data suggest how, with its cleanly distinct activity states, the prefrontal cortex may focus and keep separate the successive steps of thought: how the mental program is kept cleanly on track.

Luria's descriptions show how the programs of frontal lobe patients do not keep on track. Instead of clean, successive segments in an organized plan, behavior is blurred with a mixture of relevant and irrelevant ideas, things left undone that should be done, and things done that should not be done. Indeed, we may all be familiar with experiences of the sort that Luria describes, when we are tired, distracted, or confused. Again ideas blur; thoughts are not clearly articulated and distinguished; we do things that are only similar to what we should have done, not exactly right. In all these cases, it seems that the clean separation of cognitive enclosures has failed.

When the process works well, in contrast, we see beautiful, clear structures of thought, in which all that is relevant is assembled in just the right place. Just the right facts are present; each leads to just the right choice of action, just the correct conclusion. This is perhaps "intelligence" at its best, the intelligence that fills us with delight and admiration. Here is a literary version from Patrick O'Brian's HMS *Surprise*.

It is the middle of the Napoleonic wars. In the Indian Ocean, the *Surprise* has encountered a squadron of five French warships. The captain, Jack Aubrey, is at the masthead deliberating; as he returns to deck, the ship's surgeon sees what he describes as Aubrey's "battle-face." "On these occasions," he reflects, "my valuable friend appears to swell, actually to increase in his physical as well as his spiritual dimensions: is it an optical illusion? How I should like to measure him. The penetrating intelligence in the eye, however, is not capable of measurement."[22]

In the mind of the sea captain, many considerations must be brought to order. He cannot survive a battle with the French squadron, but neither would he wish to run directly away from them. This might bring them into the path of the merchant convoy that the *Surprise* has been set to guard; at all costs, the convoy must be protected. Deliberating at the masthead, the captain is considering his own speed and that of the French; where all ships lie with respect to the wind; the size of guns on each enemy ship and their length of fire; and, above all, the likely intentions and understanding of the rival commander, Linois. He has at his disposal his own ship and guns, and a highly trained crew; he is dragging a hidden sail beneath the water to conceal the potential speed of his vessel; he has his estimate of where the English convoy must be and how quickly the French could encounter them. He is considering that the French, after long sailing in the warm Indian Ocean, must be foul-bottomed and slow, while the *Surprise*, newly fit, is capable of exceptional speed.

Descending from the masthead, Jack Aubrey has put each of these thoughts into its place. Together they have shaped an idea: by run-

ning for awhile along a certain course, he can open a small gap in
the pursuing French line, then with a sudden reversal, he can hope
to run through this gap while keeping just out of range of the French
guns; as they turn to chase him, they will be led far away from the
sacred convoy. Everything has its exact place in this plan: the wind,
the position of the ships, their speed, the size of their guns. The plan
makes no sense without all of these thoughts correctly and precisely
assembled.

A plan has been constructed, but much still remains to be done.
All of it must be done perfectly. Jack Aubrey calls for a mango and
stands eating it as the ships fall into the pattern of the chase. He issues
the instructions that will be needed for each step of the solution: the
crew awaiting the command to come about and change sails; the best
men at the wheel; the gun holes closed along the side that will bend
into the water under the new press of sail. The move must begin at
the right second and unexpectedly, with the sudden casting off of the
hidden drag-sail. It is not mathematics or philosophy, but it is perfect
human intelligence, everything as it must be, nothing omitted. There
is no second chance.

"Still the minutes dropped by; the critical point was coming, but
slowly, slowly. Jack, motionless upon that busy deck, began to whistle
softly as he watched the far-off Linois. . . . A last glance to windward:
the forces were exactly balanced: the moment had come. He drew a
deep breath, tossed the hairy mango stone over the side, and shouted,
'Let go there.'"[23]

Chapter 7 **The Box**

We think of ourselves as reasonable beings. As discussed in chapter 1, we habitually explain our actions by the reasons that drove them. We value reason as perhaps the most human of our human characteristics. In the previous chapters we have built up a picture of what reason means in the mind and brain, as knowledge is assembled into long sequences of thought and action approaching a final goal.

Essential though it is to our view of ourselves, reason is fragile. When we say that we were distracted, tired, or forgot, we acknowledge limits to our reason. Indeed, it is interesting how very fragile reason is. Many years ago, when I was involved in research on driving safety, it was a rule of thumb that "judgment" was the first thing to suffer as blood alcohol increased. The basic skills of driving might be intact; vision and language might be fine; the driver was far from stumbling or slurring speech; but already "judgment" was starting to suffer. This corresponds to what we all experience. We must be very sleepy, drunk, or distracted indeed before we begin to see a car as a bus or turn left when we meant to turn right. But when we are only mildly tired or have had just our first glass of wine, it is already obvious that we are not thinking as clearly as we can. I sometimes wonder whether reason is so fragile because the brain mechanisms that support it have evolved so recently. The visual system, for example, is a truly solid, brass-bound piece of equipment. It is the Rolls Royce of the brain, evolved over hundreds of millions of years, time after time after time delivering a car as a car and a bus as a bus, even when they fly by in the darkness on a rainy night. The power of human reason, in contrast, is a much more recent development. It makes sense to imagine that our current reasoning system is only a first pass at a solution. Like most prototypes, it works well in confined circumstances but can easily fall apart on the road.

While tiredness and alcohol can disturb our reason, another limit is more profound. Cognitive enclosure, cognitive focus is essential to effective thought. A mental program is constructed of just the right segments, assembled into just the right structure. But this focus has another side, and in all of us, this other side is significant. Just as focus explains much of the best in our minds, it also explains much of the worst—what is most limited, and sometimes dangerous.

From chapter 5, think back to the chessboard problem and to the facts that would make it easy to solve . . . if only we found them in our minds. At all times we think inside the box. We leave latent all that knowledge that we have not brought to mind.

Very often, this means that the conclusions we draw are obviously limited or wrong. They are conclusions we never would have drawn, if only the mental focus had been different . . . if different ideas had surfaced. Like rationality, irrationality is also the product of thinking in focused, limited cognitive enclosures.

Focus is the essence of a cognitive enclosure. Just small amounts of information are assembled to solve just one small problem. In a sense, the many possible ideas we might have are competing for entry into current thinking. Attention to one thing means disregard of another.

Let me begin with some simple examples of the competition of ideas. I am starting with these because they are especially transparent; they occur only in young children and seem cute. When we see them we smile with indulgent affection, but we will see that, in our own adult reasoning, similar forces are often at play.

In the first experiment, the subjects are children aged three or four.[1] The child is sorting cards into two bins, one on the left and one on the right. Each card shows either a red star or a blue truck. The left bin is marked with a red truck, the right bin with a blue star.

The child begins with the color game. He is told that red cards go on the left and blue on the right. This game is easy. The child sorts through a pile of cards.

Now the child changes to the shape game. Now trucks go on the left, stars on the right. The experimenter checks that the child knows the rules. Sorting begins.

Of course, some children do the task fine. They put trucks on the left and stars on the right, just as they should. But at the age of three or four, many children do not do this. The videos of their performance can be extraordinary. The child picks up a red star. He says, "This is a star," and if he is asked the rules of the shape game, he can point to the right to show where the stars go. Yet when he comes to sort, he puts his red star straight into the left bin, where the red things went before. The old habit of the color game competes with the new knowledge of the shape game. While the child is answering the experimenter's question, the new knowledge is in control. But when he turns to the task and places the card, the new knowledge slips away, and the old habit reasserts its authority.

In the second example we move closer to false deduction—to

competition of ideas.[2] Again, the subjects are children about three years old. The child is shown a piece of apparatus with three open "chimneys" in a row along the top, joined by tubes to three containers in a row along the bottom. A ball can be dropped into a chimney top and will run down the tube to the container at the bottom. Tubes and containers are in plain view but opaque, so that once a ball has been dropped in, it is no longer visible as it runs to the bottom.

Balls are dropped in at the top, and the child is asked to guess where each one will end up at the bottom. In one version, the tubes go straight from top to bottom, so the leftmost chimney is joined to the leftmost container at the bottom, and so on. The children solve this version fine, always knowing where the ball will land. In another version, each tube crosses to a different place. The left chimney, for example, might connect to the middle container at the bottom. The tubes are perfectly visible; there is no ambiguity over what will happen. Still, many children cannot resist the thought that things drop vertically; they ignore the obvious tubes and always point to the container directly under the chimney that the ball went into. They can see perfectly clearly that a ball dropped into the left chimney cannot possibly arrive at the left container—but this is the container they choose. A strong thought wins; a less familiar but in this case essential consideration is ignored.

These examples seem cute, but once we look at adult thinking from this perspective, we often see something disturbingly similar. Detailed postmortems of disasters such as the nuclear accidents at Chernobyl or Three Mile Island show that operators pursued one line of thought, ignoring obvious evidence that their diagnoses were false and their attempts at correction would fail. Firefighters often explain that, in the heat of action, "only one solution came to mind"; once this solution was embarked on, no better alternative was considered. Important ideas are forced out of consideration by strong competitors.

In a reactor meltdown the costs are high and the pressure on the operator is enormous. Decisions are needed fast, without time to consider. Yet even when pressure is low and time is available, we are often blinkered by the same limitation of competing ideas. Just small fragments of the knowledge that we have are brought to mind. For now, just these fragments control our thoughts.

The experimental psychology of competing ideas is filled with examples. Often, like the children with the cards or the tubes, these examples have an entertaining irrationality. At the same time, we can feel our own minds being sucked down the same irrational path. In these examples we see many forces at work as ideas compete for control of our minds.

The first force we can examine is a kind of association of ideas. As the context of a problem changes, different ideas are made prominent. In a long and beautiful research program examining the limits of everyday reasoning, Daniel Kahneman and Amos Tversky called this "framing." Framing leads to irrational conclusions even in expert thinkers, both in laboratory tasks and in real world decisions.[3]

Here is a typical framing experiment.[4] Subjects are asked to decide between two alternative treatments for lung cancer. One is radiation therapy. The other is surgery. Subjects can be patients, doctors, or graduate students trained in statistics. All these groups behave in much the same way.

Here is the first version of the problem. Surgery is the more effective treatment, with the better long-term outcome. However, whereas nobody dies from radiation therapy, 10 percent of patients will die in surgery. Perhaps you can sense that the problem is hard to decide. In the actual experiment, about 65 percent of subjects choose surgery.

Here is the second version. Again, surgery is the more effective long-term treatment, just as it was before. As for the procedure itself, 100 percent of people survive radiation therapy, whereas 90 percent survive surgery. Now the number of subjects choosing surgery soars to 85 percent.

It does not matter that the two problems are logically the same. They sound different. In our minds, the chance of death competes for salience with the prospect of survival. To frame the problem in terms of death makes death more prominent. Even a 10 percent chance of death sounds very serious. To frame the problem in terms of survival makes survival prominent. One can be optimistic about a 90 percent chance of survival, and attention now turns to the long-term benefits of life after surgery.

The research of Kahneman and Tversky is both delightful and telling. As the cancer example shows, these psychological phenomena are compelling and significant, affecting the choices of real people casting the dice with their own lives. The cancer paper was not published in an esoteric journal of experimental psychology but for the attention of real doctors in the *New England Journal of Medicine*. We could continue with examples affecting all kinds of decision making, but two should be enough to show how powerful and pervasive such mistakes can be.[5] A salient idea comes to mind and dominates conclusions; other, essential information is ignored.

The subject is told: "Linda is 31 years old, single, outspoken and very bright. She majored in philosophy. As a student she was deeply concerned with issues of discrimination and social justice and also participated in antinuclear demonstrations."[6]

Now the subject is given various possible descriptions of Linda's current life and work. He rates how likely each one is. Mixed in among the different possible scenarios are a critical pair:

Linda is a bank teller.

Linda is a bank teller and active in the feminist movement.

Which is more probable? For 89 percent of subjects, the second scenario is rated as more likely than the first. It does not matter that this completely violates the laws of probability, in a way that is quite obvious once it is brought to mind. When the ratings are made, these laws are not brought to mind. Instead, Linda sounds very much like a feminist, and the second alternative receives an irrational boost.

The same principle is shown in the second example, this time concerning earthquake prediction. Now the subjects are professional forecasters. They estimate the probability of:

An earthquake in California causing a flood in which more than a thousand people will drown.

An earthquake somewhere in the United States in which more than a thousand people will drown.

Which is more likely? Again, the mention of California adds strength to the idea that earthquakes may occur. The laws of probability are forgotten; the first alternative is rated as more probable.

By changing what comes to mind, we can change how people think. This does not simply happen through association of ideas, as in the cancer, Linda, and earthquake examples. The same thing is seen whenever ideas become more or less accessible and thus more or less likely to affect our choices, conclusions, or preferences.

To judge how worthwhile something is, we need a standard of comparison. If different standards are brought to mind, the results can be paradoxical. Suppose a subject rates the attractiveness of different gambles. One gamble gives a certain chance, let's call it p, of winning $9. A second gives the same chance p of winning $9, but an additional chance (1-p) of losing 5 cents. Obviously the second gamble is worse, but it seems more attractive. The explicit mention of a small possible loss has increased the value of the potential gain; comparing to 5 cents has increased the value of $9. The same kind of context for comparison affects much more familiar consumer decisions. A person can drive twenty minutes to save $10 on the purchase of a pocket calculator. In one scenario the calculator costs \$25, in another \$125. Is the drive worthwhile? People are much more likely to make the drive when the cost is only \$25. In this case, saving the \$10 seems relatively important, whereas it seems trivial when the calculator already costs \$125. Both decisions feel sensible, but in both cases, it is the same twenty-minute drive, made to save exactly the same \$10.[7]

If one option has many features, many things about it can be brought to mind. This means that we can assemble reasons either to choose it or to reject it. Suppose subjects are asked to choose between two parents in a fictional custody battle.[8] They are told a lot about parent A, both good features and bad. They are told less about parent B. Asked which parent should get the child, they choose parent A. Parent A has many good points, and there is just not much to say about parent B. Now the question is changed: Which parent should be rejected? Again, the choice is parent A. Now the bad points of parent A are assembled to justify rejection; now the ignorance of parent B works to his or her advantage. Again we may say that, for parent A, the many good and bad features compete for attention. Asking which parent is fit to keep the child brings good features to the fore; asking which parent should be rejected reverses this scenario.

Of course, our daily lives are filled with choices between one option we know well and another with uncertain properties. This will usually apply, for example, with any decision to *change*—a home, a partner, a job. A colleague who is deciding to move can recite a long list of the things that have been frustrating in his or her current position; the next day, the same colleague can recite a similar long list of the things he or she loves. Meanwhile, the possible future job remains a shadowy thing of hopes, fears, and guesswork. This is a major, life-changing decision. To make it we might hope to employ all the full power of our rationality, but in a very real sense, the known and unknown options simply cannot be compared.

Sometimes information is easily available but still bizarrely ignored. Subjects are asked how much money they would pay to prevent the drowning of migratory birds. There are three versions of the problem: the money spent will save two thousand, twenty thousand, or two hundred thousand birds. How much is this worth? The amounts actually offered in the three cases are almost identical; the number, though critical, is somehow left out of consideration. Another intriguing case of neglect concerns probability, especially for choices with high emotional impact. A subject is asked how much he will pay to avoid some probability of losing twenty dollars. As the probability shifts from .01 to .99, the amount that is offered to avoid the risk increases in an eminently sensible way. Now the risk is changed; it is not losing twenty dollars but receiving a painful shock. Now the probability has almost no effect. Just one aspect of the problem—the salient pain—dominates thought, and just this one aspect determines the perceived value of escape.[9]

Ideas compete to enter the box of thought and control our conclusions. But they do not compete as individuals. Integration of mental activity appeared previously in chapter 6. A simple example is the tendency of the visual system to work simultaneously on the different properties—the color, the shape, the motion—of the same chosen object. The system is coherent; it does things that belong together. Beyond the visual system, though, the effort for coherence is among the dominant forces of thought. As ideas are assembled, our minds strive for a picture in which everything fits, in which all the pieces cohere.

Related, consistent ideas support one another's access to the box. Meanwhile, inconsistent ideas are avoided or eliminated. The principle is at once powerful and frightening. It is a method for making a mental case—any mental case—apparently invincible in its weight of supporting evidence. It makes us feel that we are right, and it is frightening because it does this so well.

Perhaps the best-known development of this principle came from the social psychologist Leon Festinger, and his theory of cognitive dissonance.[10] Incompatible ideas, Festinger proposed, lead to a sense of dissonance. When dissonance appears, the system adjusts to remove it. Beliefs can be changed; evidence can be neglected; new evidence can be sought out. The fox wants the grapes until it is clear that they will not be obtained; running off in disappointment, he reasons that those grapes were not so wonderful after all. The mind struggles until coherence is achieved.

Here is an early example of a fox-and-grapes experiment.[11] A group of women rate the desirability of a range of new household products, such as toasters and coffeemakers. (This is an experiment from the 1950s.) After the ratings, each woman is offered a choice between two things on the list; she will really get to keep the one she chooses. Then she rates again. Now, the one she chose is rated as more desirable than it was before. The one she rejected is rated as less desirable. Though it is possible to imagine various possible explanations for this result, dissonance theory would propose that beliefs have changed to become congruent with the choice.

Beliefs also change to justify effort or costs. In another early experiment, women were persuaded to join a society.[12] Though the society itself was rather dull, the initiation ceremony was not; for half the women it was something relatively mild, but for the others it was something severely embarrassing. Later, it was the women who had suffered the tough initiation who thought that the society itself was worthwhile. Perhaps only a positive view of the final benefits could justify the initial pain of joining up.

Dissonance also exerts strong pressure on the way that new evidence is interpreted. Here is a summary from one research group: "Through . . . biased assimilation even a random set of outcomes or events can appear to lend support for an entrenched position, and both sides in a given debate can have their positions bolstered by the same set of data."[13]

In their own experiment, these authors recruited two groups of subjects, one strongly in favor of capital punishment, the other strongly opposed. Both groups were exposed to the same (fictitious) research data, partly supporting and partly opposing the view that capital punishment has a significant deterrent effect. The effect of the data was to strengthen the beliefs of both groups. At the same time, each group rated the data in support of their own position as more convincing.

Evidence may not just be selectively interpreted: evidence congruent with our actions may be actively sought out. In another experiment, high school students read information about a fictitious employee, Mr. Miller.[14] Miller had been hired six months earlier as the manager of a fashion store, and a number of reports were available on his performance. Each of the student subjects was now to decide whether Miller's contract should be extended. Subjects were told how important it is to evaluate others correctly and that some people are better at this than others. Once the information had been digested and their decision made, the subjects were given a chance to look over several additional reports from Miller's colleagues. Some were favorable, some unfavorable. Even if there was no chance that the decision could be changed, subjects were biased in the reports they chose to read. If they had opted for termination, they were now more likely to read negative reports. If they had opted for extension, they instead sought further evidence of Miller's successes. Nothing they read now could change Miller's fate; nothing could change the decision that the experimenter had already recorded. Subjects were doing this for no practical reason—simply to back up their decisions in their own minds.

Beyond the colorful world of the dissonance experiments, the pressure toward consistency surfaces in many forms. It does not just affect decisions to join exotic artificial societies or to terminate fictitious employees. It influences many kinds of decisions, feelings, and beliefs.

People believe, for example, that costs and benefits are negatively correlated; if perceived benefits increase, then perceived risks go down.[15] The phenomenon may be important whenever costs and benefits must be balanced: when people decide whether to live close to a nuclear power plant, whether to employ safe sex, whether to take up smoking. It means, for example, that an advertisement suggesting positive benefits from smoking—from the dreamy enjoyment of a small cigar to the coolness of a shared cigarette in a bar—is not just promoting these benefits. By the principle of consistency, it is also likely to reduce the expected cost. As one set of ideas wins the struggle for control of our thoughts, the rival set is exterminated.

In the world of mental competition, one of the great players is surely emotion. How often, infuriated with a sulky teenager or resentful of our partner, have we thought, "What does s/he *ever* do for me?" At that moment, I have sometimes paused to realize that, right at this moment, I actually cannot answer the question—right at this moment, I really cannot bring to mind all the things that s/he does, every day, to make my life worthwhile. This is mental focus—the dominance of a congruent set of current thoughts—written large indeed. Just for this moment, only anger dominates, and only thoughts consistent with that anger can surface. As the Monty Python team express it so perfectly in *Life of Brian*, "What have the Romans ever done for us?"

Anger, love, happiness, and misery all color our thoughts with the rationalizations of the moment. Depression is a spiral, not just because the person feels hopeless and worthless, but also because the sense of worthlessness brings only added thoughts of worthlessness to mind.[16] Our estimates of potential dangers are irrationally biased by the strength of the fear we feel: when fear is strong, the danger seems probable and real, but as fear abates, our beliefs, choices, and preferences change. People fear air crashes more than car accidents—but by a huge margin, it is car accidents that get them in the end. People will pay more for flight insurance that covers "death from a terrorist attack" than for insurance covering death from all causes![17] The thought of a terrorist brings up the thought of danger and death, and suddenly, the danger and death seem real. Parents imagine pedophiles in the street, but it is the cars in the street, not the pedophiles, that their children have really to fear.

In the 9/11 attacks, more than three thousand people lost their lives. For family and friends, each one of those losses was an individual tragedy. But roughly speaking, around 2.5 million Americans die each year, or around seven thousand every day.[18] Each of these deaths is also an individual loss, and many of the causes—smoking, traffic accidents, undiagnosed breast cancer—are at least as avoidable as terrorist attacks and are killers on a far greater scale. How much should Americans fear the consequences of that single day? How much should be spent to prevent similar days in the future?

With different contexts, very different answers seem natural. Perhaps six months after the 9/11 attacks, I visited family in the United States and was astounded, when a news program appeared on television, to see written across the bottom of the screen: "Attack on America—Day 185." (It may not have been 185—but it was a large number.) For a foreigner, exposed to foreign media, a shocking attack on America had come and gone; for Americans, exposed to American media, anger and fear were kept simmering and alive. Both perspectives, of course, have their dangers as well as their strengths. Both are our own cognitive inventions, with the strength of what they foreground, the danger of what they omit.

It is a small step from emotional to social bias, and to the classic boys' camp experiments of the 1950s.[19] In these experiments, ordinary boys attended a summer camp. At random, the experimenters divided the boys into two groups, housed in separate bunkhouses. After a week of harmony, the experimenters began a series of competitions between the two bunkhouse groups. The competitions were only games, but with points, prizes, and a final trophy, the experimenters made sure that both groups were determined to come out the winners.

Fairly soon, relations between the bunkhouse groups degenerated to open hostility, with flag burning, raids on one another's houses, and so on. Boys rated members of their own group as "friendly, tough, brave," but members of the other group as "sneaky, smart alecks, stinkers." Of course, these were random groups of human beings, put together by the accident of the experiment. It is the same person who is tough if he happens to be in our group but a stinker if he happens to be in the other.

Again, the experiments showed how group membership biases many aspects of cognition. For example: Boys were set to compete on a bean collecting game. When the game was over, each boy was shown the beans collected by every player and asked to estimate the number. Two prizes were available: one for the most beans collected, and one for the best estimates. Despite this reward for accurate estimation, boys judged that their own group members had done better. Even looking directly at the beans, they thought that their own group members had collected more.

Perhaps there are few such universal biases as our tendency to judge people, events, and things as universally "good" or "bad." If something is good in one way, we see it as good in others, as if the whole universe were composed of just two categories of entities, those we are for and those we are against. Of course, the universe is not constructed this way. From individuals to political systems to events, the universe is composed of entities with many properties, some of these properties (by our lights) good, others bad. We know it but often struggle to remember it.

We believe in our reason, but reason is not what we are seeing in these examples. What we are seeing is rationalization. It is not a world in which evidence leads to conclusions. It is a world in which conclusions are chosen, and evidence is then assembled in support.

Once the pattern is recognized, we see it in many facets of our thinking. We use reason to plan a day at the beach, deciding on travel plans, what we need to take, and how long we can spend. We use reason to repair a bicycle, to get the children ready for bed, or to develop a proof in formal logic. But for many complex problems, at work, at home, in politics, and in relationships, all too often reason seems the exception, rationalization the rule. We do not hold our political views because we can prove in any convincing way that they are right. We hold our views and assemble around them a set of advantages that are consistent with their being right. We do not admire our own children because they are especially admirable. We admire our children and then think often of the things they do well. Around the world, many millions of people believe passionately in the rightness of their own religion, but this is not because one religion is in general preferable to others. Usually, the particular religion is determined by the accident of birthplace, but a lifetime is then spent in a context of supporting arguments. To believe otherwise is to believe that all those countless of millions of other people, with other political views, other children, other religions, are bizarrely wrong. Of course they are not wrong; they are just like ourselves, but with the brain's force of rationalization focused around a different set of beliefs and conclusions.

In reason, a step is taken because one fact implies another. The side-angle-side rule does not have something loosely to do with congruency of triangles; if the rule can be shown to be satisfied, then the triangles are congruent. But as we construct the much looser stories of rationalization, one idea can support another simply because, in some much weaker sense, they seem to belong together. It does not follow that, because we cannot have the grapes, we did not want them. This just makes a more emotionally congruent story. As we watch the cool young woman lighting her cigarette, it does not seem possible that, at the same time, she is increasing her chance of emphysema.

In chapter 1, I quoted Francis Bacon's case for reason: "Ipsa scientia potestas est." But Bacon also firmly recognized the lure of rationalization: "The human understanding when it has once adopted an opinion draws all things else to support and agree with it. And though there be a greater number and weight of instances to be found on the other side, yet these it either neglects and despises, or else by some distinction sets aside and rejects, in order that by this great and pernicious predetermination the authority of its former conclusion may remain inviolate."[20]

True reason depends on knowledge of the world. It depends on knowing that X implies Y, so that if X has been established, Y can be concluded. Earlier I argued that, to a large degree, science is simply our normal process of acquiring knowledge, and our normal process of reasoning with that knowledge, made more systematic.

We also need not look far for a stylized and perfected version of rationalization. The essence of rationalization is the careful assembly of just one side of the argument. It is used in any debate or court of law, but to see its full power, we need only listen to any radio or television interview with a modern politician.

It is transparent, but astonishingly, it works. It is invariably obvious that, before the interview, the politician has decided that arguments A, B, and C support his or her position, whereas arguments 1, 2, and 3 oppose it. The strategy is then simple. Arguments A, B, and C are repeated as many times as possible. No matter how often the interviewer tries to introduce arguments 1, 2, and 3, these are belittled or simply ignored. The interviewer says, "Let me ask you about 3." The politician replies, "I would like to repeat what I said about C." It is embarrassing in its superficiality, bias, and blatant refusal to deliver a balanced analysis. We know what is being done to us. Yet still, it works: A, B, and C gain access to our cognitive enclosures, and 1, 2, and 3 are suppressed.

Here is a beautiful summary of the power of the method. It may sound chillingly familiar, especially when we hear its source:

> Naturally the common people don't want war: Neither in Russia, nor in England, nor for that matter in Germany. That is understood. But, after all, it is the leaders of the country who determine the policy and it is always a simple matter to drag the people along, whether it is a democracy, or a fascist dictatorship, or a parliament, or a communist dictatorship. Voice or no voice, the people can always be brought to the bidding of the leaders. That is easy. All you have to do is tell them they are being attacked, and denounce the peacemakers for lack of patriotism and exposing the country to danger. It works the same in any country.

The speaker is Hermann Göring at Nuremberg.[21]

To take a more recent example, Tony Blair once famously declared that he had "complete inner confidence" in his policies for the Middle East. One may have different opinions about the occupation of Iraq, but in a situation of such complexity and confusion, so filled with ethical dilemmas and factual uncertainties, it seems safe to say that the one thing that is not justified is "complete inner confidence." Only Blair can know whether this inner confidence was real or whether, in saying this, he wished to promote complete inner confidence in his audience. Either way, either in Blair or in his listeners, it seems that any such confidence could be achieved only by the full power of mental bias, by the systematic mental assembly of one side of the case.

I sometimes wonder how a politician feels at the end of a long session in front of the cameras. Does he or she leave with the sense of a job well done, or instead does the politician long, just once, to be allowed to tell the truth as he or she sees it—to give the public an intelligent, balanced account of a complex, uncertain issue?

As I said earlier, a trademark of rationalization is loose association of ideas. Fact A does not really imply fact B; the two just go well together, so that believing one encourages us to believe the other. This principle of loose association is used to devastating effect in building the one-sided cases of politics. A rival's views on abortion may suddenly, absurdly be introduced into a debate on economic control. It does not matter that these two sets of issues are entirely independent. In our own minds, the different views of one individual are linked— if we doubt him or her on X, we may also tend to doubt him or her on Y. In fact, I have always found it extraordinary that we seem able to bundle so many separate sets of ideas under a generic heading of "right" or "left." Abortion, health care, oil drilling in Alaska, taxation, and the existence of God are all vital, elaborate, complex issues in their own right. To form a view on any one of these must be a complex and detailed matter, and for the different issues, the complexities and details are quite independent.

Of course, we live not just with our own one-sided ideas but in one-sided subcultures. As a scientist, I have perhaps not met one American academic—not one—who voted for George Bush. Recently, I spent a few days with a great friend, among the most gentle of men

I have ever met, in Santa Fe, New Mexico. He thought it quite unsurprising that academics would not vote for Bush. His reason was that the people who voted for Bush were "idiots."

When I quizzed him on that, he took back the "idiots," but that was what first came to mind. When I first lived in the United States, in Eugene, Oregon, in 1976, it was fashionable for young Europeans to mock the political ignorance of Americans. We loved to believe that Americans knew nothing outside their own city limits, and when I reached Oregon, the *Eugene Register-Guard* did little to change my mind. Visiting friends in Eugene thirty years later, I happened to turn to the letter page of the *Register-Guard*. I was stunned, not only by the depth of political information and conviction but also by the raw scorn of opposing views that now dripped from the page. It is often said that American politics has become increasingly polarized; if the *Register-Guard* is anything to go by, that is putting it mildly.

In my view, few voters are idiots. But one-sided thinking is a frightening power, with the potential to make idiots of us all. This may be increasingly dangerous as our exposure to information itself becomes more and more one-sided—from communities of like-minded friends, from members of the same church, from television stations with their own political bias. Back with my friends in Santa Fe, the conversation turned to another member of the group, who works as a social studies teacher in a Colorado high school. She said that, in social studies class, children really love the political debates . . . for one of the few times in modern American life, they get to discuss real issues, not with pundits, pastors, or parents, but with an actual cross-section of normal, real people with their own, individual minds. With a newspaper or a television program, we perhaps have too much control . . . if the arguments do not appeal, we can press a button and change the channel. Perhaps this makes it all too easy to stay trapped in our own, one-sided mental creations. Especially when they do not agree with us, perhaps one great advantage of real, other people is that they are not so easy to turn off.

Evidently, mental bias is a loss. When we rationalize, we learn nothing from the facts. There is no reason, balance, breadth of understanding. Jack Aubrey, on the deck of HMS Surprise, cannot survive by disregarding any facts that would doom his plan. We cannot get to work by ignoring the empty tank of the car, and we cannot prove a theorem simply by writing QED.

The loss is especially stark when we consider that, in many cases, the same facts can lead different, equally sensible people to opposite, equally strong conclusions. Think back to the capital punishment study or to the many millions of people born into different cultures and, by this accident, destined to have opposing religious beliefs. If views do not follow from facts, what is the point of forming views at all?

Thinking about this through a long lifetime of difficult decisions—which line of work to pursue, which city to live in, whether to move house, when to have children—I have come to believe that, biased and foolish though it certainly is, rationalization may have a function. For many of life's most difficult decisions, we simply do not know which option is "best." Many of the facts are not available. Much depends on the uncertainty of the future. Often we are balancing considerations that simply cannot be compared—the importance of the next career step against the unknown joys of a first baby. Reason is of little help here. We do not have the facts to reason with.

Still, we cannot do nothing. In life's big decisions, the key thing is not simply to choose what is best. The key thing, I have come to believe, is to choose *something* and intend to make it work out. On this perspective, a choice is also a commitment. Our choices do not work for us simply because they were made wisely. Just as important, they work because we commit to making this happen.

From this perspective, we may see a merit of fallible, foolish, one-sided thinking. For commitment we need confidence, an unswerving faith that we are right, a decision to back our choices and our conclusions *no matter what*. Perhaps, when problems are too uncertain to be truly solved, rationalization can fill the gap—with a conclusion we believe, though for no good reason. Dangerous though this can be, it may sometimes help when any decision is better than no decision at all.

Of course, the bias to consistency is just a force in mental competition. It is not an irresistible force, and when we strive to see both sides of an argument, or when the opposite view is forced into awareness, even the most entrenched beliefs can be challenged or overturned. In an early smoking study, young smokers volunteered to act the part of a person with cancer. The task required the subject to build a detailed antismoking case, and even eighteen months later, these subjects were still smoking less. In the Korean War, this kind of elaboration of the competing view was a method of indoctrination used on American prisoners of war. If a prisoner could once be made to agree that American society was not perfect, later he was encouraged to explain and develop that doubt, in ever greater depth. In our own mental life, we do a milder version of the same thing. When we hear a case against what we believe, we try to remember that we should listen, see both sides, keep an open mind. We try to remember this because, like Bacon, we know it is often so hard.[22]

Often, experiments on mental bias show the importance of the context. If people are asked to rate their general happiness, they are badly affected by rain; they are less happy today because of the bad weather, and this momentary feeling spills over into what they believe of their happiness in general. This effect is eliminated, though, if they are first asked about the weather, perhaps reminding them that today's feeling is just a mood. In the problem of Linda the feminist, things can improve, at least for the statistically trained, if the problem is reworded to bring this training explicitly to mind. Jurors' first judgments can be heavily influenced by the sense of outrage that they feel, but instruction to consider other factors can balance this emotional response. Mental balance may sometimes be elusive, but forces can be marshaled in its favor.[23]

There is another great player in mental competition. This is the force of habit—our tendency to do the same things today that we did yesterday and the day before that. Habits are formed at every level of thought, from the skills of tying a shoelace to the life plans we choose to pursue. Again I am often struck, both by the power this gives us and by how unreasonable it can appear.

Most of us spend day after day, week after week, year after year in dogged pursuit of the same long-term goals at home and work. Sometimes, waking up in the morning I am reminded of a computer booting up, as the same bits of software come into control of my plans and concerns for the day—the routine of getting up and getting ready to leave the house, the children to be fed, the unfinished business from the previous day at work. Of course I value these things, and without this dogged running down the same tracks, no long-term goal would ever be achieved. But is this why these things take control of my day? Is it really the value that drives my choices?

Equally plausibly, it is all just a habit. I do these things, not because each day I have reflected and chosen to do them, but because I did them yesterday. Just a brief weekend's holiday in Venice makes this immediately clear. Things that, back in Cambridge, seemed overwhelmingly consuming—things I could not possibly get off my mind—suddenly have faded into the background. Of course, if I think about those things then I care about them again, but the fact is, I do not think about them. Instead the habit is broken, and my mind is free to marvel at a Bellini painting.

Though the force of habit is doubtless indispensable, it seems likely that, for most of us, the balance is wrong. As the joke goes, nobody ever said on their deathbed, "I wish I'd spent another day at the office." Many years ago, when I was living in the United States, my wife and I had taken the children to a typical featureless, characterless, immeasurably tedious American shopping mall. (I hate shopping.) At a clothing store, she took our five-year-old son inside to buy jeans; I stayed outside to look after our second lovely young boy, aged about eighteen months. To entertain each other, soon we were chasing round and round some sign planted in the middle of the mall. We were both screaming with laughter; sitting next to us on a bench, an old man was watching us and soon beaming, too. It was a moment of free, unrestricted joy, for the father who chased, for the boy who was chased, for the man who watched. But how often do we plan for a day, an hour, or even a minute of such joy?

Years later, my older, by then politically concerned son was holding forth against mindless capitalism. He believed that a successful businessman or woman continues to pursue wealth long after it makes sense to do so. He said, "Let's face it, Dad—after your first hundred million, no more can possibly make any difference." Although I thought the amount was comical, the principle seems sound enough. Though people in general believe that more money will make them happier, the real effects of increasing income are often transitory, and barely visible at all if, instead of simply asking people how happy they think they are, a detailed attempt is made to measure actual happiness at different times of an actual day. Meanwhile, buying into the goal of financial success does its own harm; the person who is most motivated by money tends overall to be less satisfied with family, friendships, and life. In part, we care for goals that really do matter, but in part, we fall into conventional habits of mind. Doubtless it would be a disaster to deliberate about the best use of each little moment of each little day. For many of us, though, it could be that a little more deliberation would be no bad thing.[24]

In previous chapters, I showed how cognitive enclosure lies at the heart of human intelligence. By systematic solution of focused subproblems, we achieve effective, goal-directed thought and behavior.

This chapter has shown another side of enclosure. Limits to human reason, as well as human intelligence, come from enclosed thinking. As a problem is assessed, ideas compete for consideration. Essential knowledge, available though it may be, remains dormant and ignored. At the extreme, reason descends into rationalization. A small, apparently coherent body of thought assumes control; its rivals, perhaps leading to quite different conclusions, are suppressed.

This, certainly, is a weakness in each of us. It is a fundamental fragility, one that can blind us to balance and to truth. The power of reason gives us our greatest intellectual achievements, from mathematics to the conduct of the *Surprise*. Its fragility gives us our greatest failures of neglected evidence and unjustified certainty.

Chapter 8 **The One Sure Thing**

T here is a risk to avoid in popular science. This is the atmosphere of unquestioned authority; the scientist explains, the reader learns. Science, though, is always provisional, not a final truth, and the adventure lies in the process, the struggle for understanding. When science is explained, the things that are explained are ideas and the observations on which those ideas are based. Ideas develop; ideas should always be questioned. In science as in life, the one sure thing is change.

At the heart of human intelligence, I have suggested, is the multiple-demand system of the frontal and parietal lobes. Its function is to assemble the structured mental programs of thought. A program is a series of cognitive enclosures, each dedicated to the solution of one focused subproblem. In a sense, the cognitive enclosure is analogous to the innate releasing mechanism/IRM of instinctive animal behavior. Just as a sequence of IRMs controls a complex structure of behavior in a mating stickleback or a hunting toad, so a sequence of cognitive enclosures controls our own structured thought and behavior, from the actors in the Havana plaza to Jack Aubrey aboard HMS *Surprise*. In contrast, though, to the fixed content and operations of the IRM, the contents of a human cognitive enclosure have immense flexibility, assembling any information we can possess, at any level of abstraction, in pursuit of any goal we can imagine. My story has dealt with the basis for g and for traditional "intelligence" testing. In the insights provided by thinking computers, the story has covered much in the mystery of human thought—problem solving, insight, the chain of inference. At the same time, these ideas address many of thought's failures, as knowledge competes to control our conclusions, opinions, and beliefs.

A century from now, how much of this story—the creation of cognitive enclosures, the multiple-demand system and its role in g, the link from artificial to human intelligence—will remain? It is a good story, and I would be disappointed as well as surprised to see it vanish altogether. It is perhaps unusual for scientific knowledge simply to be replaced; instead, as ideas evolve, older versions can be seen to have been approximations, good to a degree, but limited in their scope and accuracy. This would be my hope for current ideas on the human mind and brain. As knowledge accumulates, I should expect the thinking of 2010 to seem increasingly approximate. Like an early map of the globe, many contours are distorted, and many large areas labeled simply "unknown." Imperfect though it is, however, the map is already usable. We expect later versions to be much better, but not completely different.

The understanding of today depends on the insights of great twentieth-century thinkers: Charles Spearman, Aleksandr Luria, Allen Newell, and others. At the same time, this field is moving rapidly, and the book I write today has already moved forward from the book that could have been written in 2000 or even 2005. A serious convergence of experimental psychology, functional brain imaging, neurophysiology, and artificial intelligence has never been possible until today. How is the story moving and changing now?

❖

Puzzles like Raven's Matrices measure something important about the mind. This is shown by their strong relationship to *g*, their reliance on the brain's multiple-demand system, and their link to the mental programming deficits of frontal lobe patients. Still, it can be hard to design experiments using such complex tasks, where the subject is left to create his own strategy and plan of attack. Though we may guess, often we do not know exactly what a subject is doing as he works on a matrix problem.

A better chance might be a more constrained task that is still strongly correlated with puzzles like Raven's Matrices. The correlation suggests that important processing operations are the same. In the more tightly controlled task, though, they may be easier to investigate.

In chapter 4, I described the London Transport experiments and the bizarre errors they can produce. Like frontal lobe patients, some subjects may describe the rules of a new task correctly yet completely fail to obey them. In most cases, the subjects who do this also score poorly on a test such as the Raven. In current experiments, we are asking what happens as new task rules are learned. What happens as a person assembles a new, structured mental program?

A typical experiment works like this. The subject has several rules to learn. For example, two pictures appear on a screen, one above the other. Between them is an arrow pointing left or right. Rules might be:

If the pictures are crossed out, press a key with the left hand. Otherwise:

If neither picture is a bird, do nothing.

If one picture is a bird, look at the arrow. Press one of two keys with the right hand depending on which way the arrow is pointing.

If both pictures are birds, do nothing.

In the experiments described in chapter 4, the rules concerned other task events—letters and numbers flashing on a screen, and instructions showing which side to watch. We are now fairly sure that it does not matter what the rules are. What matters is that the subject has several rules to learn before the task is begun, like learning the rules of a new card game. It is this combination of separate rules that overloads the system and brings out the strange mismatch between what is known and what is done.

What must happen as new rules are learned? The subject must establish a new internal control structure: a set of cognitive enclosures that can trigger the correct response for each different display. We might imagine, though we do not know, that each enclosure must be built within the brain's multiple-demand system—perhaps as one of those independent patterns of neural activity that are seen for different parts of one task in the monkey experiments.

In a typical experiment, most subjects can do well with just one or two rules. But as the number of rules increases, the system begins to struggle. Not unlike with Luria's frontal lobe patients, the rules begin to blur, jumble, or vanish. As in the experiments of chapter 4, the rules may still be there if we stop the task and ask the subject to repeat them. It is when the subject tries to use these rules that the structure collapses.

Once again, all of this is linked closely to g. As the number of rules increases, difficulties appear in more and more subjects. At any one level of difficulty, though, it is the people with the lower g scores who struggle most. The experiments link g to a specific limit on mental capacity: the complexity, or the number of cognitive enclosures to be assembled, in a new mental program.[1]

Here is an even newer set of results. I still only half-believe this finding; in a way it seems too good to be true, and it will certainly take more experiments to confirm it. The thought is this. How does the mind assemble a new set of cognitive enclosures? Each one must be clear, distinct, containing just the right information for this specific rule. As the number of rules goes up, the sense is that, in the subject's mind, the structure begins to blur. As a friend of mine, Tom Manly, once put it, it is as though the whole thing collapses into a soup of unstructured ideas. (Tom is interested in rehabilitation of cognitive functions after brain injury, and in brain injury, this sense of a soup can be very striking.)

If this is true, we reasoned, could our subjects be helped to impose order on the soup? More exactly, could they be helped to help themselves? So far we have one set of results on this, using the old letters and numbers task from chapter 4. As usual the rules are explained: Subjects are told that each trial has two streams of letters and numbers, one to the left and one to the right; they are told they should repeat letters out loud but ignore numbers; they are told to watch only one side at a time; they are told about the cues indicating which side to watch. Then, before they actually begin on the task, they are split into two groups. One group is asked merely to repeat back the rules. They explain what they have to do, and then the task begins. The other group is asked to do the same thing, but instead of describing the rules any way they like, they are asked to give them back as a series of separate bullet points. We are trying to force subjects to organize the soup—to form separate, distinct cognitive enclosures. And at least in this first experiment, it works. In the first condition, with free-form explanation of the rules, subjects with low g scores run into trouble. In the second condition, with bullet points, this is much less true. Now everybody, high or low g, does equally well.

In one way, this seems believable. Certainly, as we struggle with new problems, from assembling mail-order furniture to using a new DVD recorder, mastery often comes as we impose order—as distinct pieces of the puzzle are identified and set apart. But can people really be made to do this better simply by asking? Can we instruct a general strategy for intelligence?

It is a wonderful idea, and these first results are certainly promising. This would not be the first time, however, that I have been wildly misled by early, promising results. An Italian student of mine used to hate it when I used the word "promising," because she had come to regard it as the death knell for the future of her projects. For the bullet points we need more time and more experiments.

In functional MRI experiments, one full scan of the brain takes one to two seconds. In this scan, activity is separately measured for thousands of small cubes of brain, stacked together to make up the whole brain volume. A typical cube may represent the activity of a few million neurons. In a typical experiment, many scans are taken in turn, over a block of perhaps five minutes. Over this five-minute block, we see how changes in brain activity follow changes in the subject's task.

It is certainly very coarse to average together the activity of several million neurons, between them doing many different things. It may show that a particular region of the brain is involved in some rather general function, such as recognizing faces or generating speech. It is less useful for making finer distinctions, such as recognition of a particular face or production of a particular word. Within the millions of neurons of one brain cube, it is not likely that most cells will be dedicated to just one face or one word. Obviously enough, if this happened we would quickly be out of cubes. Instead, what happens is that each cube has neurons responding to many different faces, and complementarily, neurons for any one face are distributed across many cubes. So all faces produce some activity across the whole face-processing area, and in general terms, the activity pattern for different faces is very much the same.

Very much the same . . . but perhaps, not identical? A new way is now developing for analysis of functional MRI data. Suppose we have two mental events (perhaps two faces), A and B. Across some area of brain (perhaps a face-processing area), each small cube will have some A neurons (neurons that respond more strongly to A than to B) and some B neurons. But by chance, it may be that, in any one person's brain, the proportions of A and B neurons vary somewhat from cube to cube. Some cubes have a slight preference for A, others for B, still others no preference either way. If we look at the exact pattern of activity in one person's brain, we may in a sense be able to read his or her mind—we may know whether, at this moment, he or she is looking at A or B or perhaps even just thinking of A or B.[2]

This may seem far-fetched, with millions of separate neurons in each cube. It is more plausible, though, because neurons in the brain tend somewhat to clump together, with nearby cells having similar properties. In any case, far-fetched or not, it can be made to work. In many parts of the brain, the exact pattern of activity can be used to read many details of the person's current task or thought. We have used this approach ourselves to examine activity in the visual system and determine whether the subject is creating a mental image of the letter X or O.[3]

Can the same method be used to examine information coding in the multiple-demand system? From monkey neurophysiology, we expect coding of all kinds of task-relevant information, and already results are beginning to suggest the same in the human brain. Here, for example, is a striking piece of mind reading.[4] On each trial, the subject will be shown a number. In advance, he is asked to decide whether he will add one to the number or subtract one from it. It is up to him; all he is told is to mix together some addition and some subtraction trials. Now the experimenter examines the pattern of brain activity before the number actually appears—when the subject has decided what to do but has not yet done it. Perhaps we may think that the chosen rule, or the corresponding cognitive enclosure, is already established in the multiple-demand system. If so, the activity pattern at this point should predict what will happen, either add or subtract, when the number finally appears—and indeed, it does.

This remarkable opportunity to examine the fine detail of human brain activity suggests many questions. The prediction would be, for example, that when color is relevant to the subject's task, the multiple-demand system codes color, but when the task changes to recognizing shapes, the multiple-demand system follows suit and codes shape. Can this new method show us how cleanly the pattern of multiple-demand activity separates a task's different rules or stages? Can we see changes in this clean separation as the task increases in complexity? Or with changes in g? Or as a person becomes distracted or sleepy? Brain imaging will never have the detail of single cell physiology, but with experiments like this, it moves a significant step closer.

In his account of frontal lobe patients, Luria often distinguished between active and passive behavior. In normal subjects, he proposed, the mind actively probes for solutions to its problems, by organizing, searching, evaluating. In frontal lobe patients, this is replaced by passivity and inertia—an easy or familiar solution, often with no real chance of success. Passivity is striking when a patient knows what should be done yet makes no apparent attempt to do it. Somehow, the failure gets lost in the patient's mind; it generates no new idea, no new attempt at resolution.

In a fascinating paper, Donald Norman and Tim Shallice made this the heart of an explanation for frontal lobe functions.[5] Behavior, they suggested, can be controlled by two parallel routes in the brain. One route is available for familiar, practiced routines and habits, such as tying one's shoelaces, reading a sentence out loud, or traveling to work. This route is accompanied by a sense of effortlessness; it is as though the task does itself. The second route is brought into play when the task is unfamiliar, difficult, or dangerous. This route involves the frontal lobes. It is accompanied by a sense of active control, by a sense of individual attention and will.

The history of experimental psychology shows many related ideas. Intuitively, it is obvious that practiced and unpracticed tasks are controlled in a very different way: the student driver concentrates carefully on every move of the controls, whereas twenty years later, the same person may be almost unaware of what he or she is doing. Experiments confirm this change in attentional demand. When we concentrate on a new task, it is impossible to do something else at the same time. As the same task becomes familiar and routine, it seems to run on autopilot, leaving attention free for other activities. Sometimes, experts may no longer be able to describe what it is they do—for example, how their fingers move across a keyboard or how they tie their shoelaces.[6]

What is the relation between novel and familiar mental programs? What change happens as the same program is run again and again? In line with the ideas of Norman and Shallice, functional MRI experiments show reduced activity across the multiple-demand system when simple, repetitive tasks become familiar and automatic.[7] This is not to say, though, that all such activity is eliminated; and in monkey experiments, many frontal neurons code task events even after months or years of training. Something similar applies to g correlations. Novelty, of course, is characteristic of typical fluid intelligence tests such as Raven's Matrices. In puzzles of this sort, each problem is different from the one before. Each one, in a sense, requires a new mental structure to be assembled, a new set of issues to be considered and addressed. This is quite different from the simple, repetitive tasks of much experimental psychology, where for hundreds of trials, subjects make much the same responses to much the same stimuli and events. In line with the idea that novelty is important, training in a simple task may reduce its correlation with g. Again, though, the correlation does not fully disappear.[8]

In terms of brain systems, there are several possibilities for thinking about these results. One is that, as a task becomes highly familiar, essentially the same brain systems remain in play, but perhaps operating in a more robust way, less sensitive to such disturbances as divided attention. A second possibility, more in line with the ideas of Norman and Shallice, is gradual transfer of control to a different system. A third is also appealing. Movements of our body are controlled by many parallel systems in the brain and spinal cord, somehow coordinated and integrated. Perhaps the same applies to mental as well as movement programs, so that as learning develops, there is increasing reliance on multiple, parallel routes of control for the same mental activity.

Here is one intriguing result that supports this line of thought. Recall our experiments in which the monkey watches a series of pictures, awaiting a specific target. After training in this task, many frontal neurons act as target detectors, giving little response to the series of nontargets but strong responses when the target finally appears. Now we ask what these same cells do when the monkey makes a mistake. Occasionally, he treats the nontarget as a target, making the eye movement that he is supposed to withhold until the target appears. When this error happens, though, the frontal target detector cells do not respond. The monkey made a mistake, but these frontal cells did not, as if this mistake was generated in some other part of the brain. The same result is seen in experiments with two streams of pictures shown on different sides of the screen. By a cue at the start of each trial, the monkey is instructed to pay attention just to one side, responding only to a target on that side. He is good with this instruction, but not perfect; occasionally, he ignores it and responds to a target on the wrong side. Again, though, whatever does this, it is not the monkey's prefrontal target detectors. They obey the instruction and remain silent.[9]

Certainly, important changes occur as the same mental program is repeated, over minutes, days, or many years. Certainly, too, the multiple-demand system does not work alone in control and execution of a mental program. In chapter 6 we discussed integration between brain systems and the construction of coherent brain activity directed to a common goal. Very likely, to understand learning we must also understand integration.

With his concept of g, Spearman aimed to explain universal positive correlations among different cognitive activities. Tests of reasoning, memory, language, spatial thinking, sensory discrimination . . . in all cases, good performance on one tends also to go with good performance on others. Spearman's explanation is some common factor, contributing to success in all kinds of tasks.

At the heart of g, on my story, there is the multiple-demand system and its role in assembly of a mental program. In any task, no matter what its content, there is a sequence of cognitive enclosures, corresponding to the different steps of task performance. For any task, the sequence can be composed well or poorly. In a good program, important steps are cleanly defined and separated, false moves avoided. If the program is poor, the successive steps may blur, become confused or mixed. In the disorganized behavior of frontal lobe patients, we see this risk in all tasks, in all that we do. We see that the brain needs constant vigilance to keep thought and behavior on track. A system organizing behavior in this way will certainly contribute to all kinds of tasks, and if its efficiency varies across people, it will produce universal positive correlations.

The importance of multiple-demand activity in such tests as Raven's Matrices—activity in this same system for tasks of many kinds—the role of this system in creating cognitive enclosures, and the importance of accurate mental programming in all tasks: all of these give strong support to this explanation for g. But is it the only explanation? Might other factors also contribute to universal positive correlations?

Though we do not know the answer, we certainly have reasons to wonder. A long-lasting debate has asked whether g derives primarily from genes or from environment, and as in most such debates, the answer is certainly that there is some of each. On the environment side, for example, intriguing results suggest that performance on Raven's Matrices may improve after intensive training on short-term memory tasks like backwards recall of a telephone number.[10] Meanwhile, the search is on for genes that influence g, and though this work is only beginning, some answers are starting to appear. Most likely, there will not be one or a few genes with large influences on g. Instead, there will be many genes, each with a small influence. Furthermore, it seems unlikely that genes will affect only specific brain systems, such as the multiple-demand system. Instead, genes are likely to have rather general effects, throughout and even outside the nervous system.[11]

This suggests another reason for universal positive correlations. This time, we are not imagining that all tasks make common demands on the same cognitive or brain function. Instead, we are imagining that, throughout the brain, all functions are likely to be affected by the same genes, with the same broad effects on neural development.

The two explanations might be combined in several ways. One possibility is that positive correlations arise for essentially different reasons—partly because of common multiple-demand involvement in all different tasks, partly because of shared genetic (or other) influences on many different parts of the brain. Or the two explanations could be linked. For example, it could be that, among many brain functions, it is multiple-demand functions that are most affected by genetic variations, so that tests of these functions, such as Raven's Matrices, are the best measures of g. It is also possible that several factors lead to positive correlations, but that in practice, some are much more significant than others.

I think I can see how these explanations could be distinguished, but for now this is a thought experiment, not practically feasible without very large numbers of brain-damaged patients. Suppose we assemble a large group of patients with damage specifically restricted to the multiple-demand system. Obviously—and as our data already show—these patients will be impaired in a standard measure of g, such as Raven's Matrices. But what will happen in other tasks? If g is largely a matter of multiple-demand contribution to all possible tasks, then all tasks should be correspondingly impaired. If this is all there is to it, in fact, we can calculate exactly how much every possible task should be impaired, based on its particular g correlation. But if g is a matter of common influence on development of many separate brain systems, the multiple-demand lesion does not reduce g for all tasks. Most brain systems are left intact, and our calculation of how much each task should suffer from a reduction in g will go wrong.

As I say, this is a thought experiment and in practice would be difficult to achieve. Certainly we should expect to learn much more as the development of the nervous system, with both its genetic and its environmental influences, is increasingly understood. For now, I think we can be confident that multiple-demand activity is one important explanation for g. Perhaps, though, it is not the whole explanation.

A fascinating question is the relationship between intelligence and wisdom. In common experience, we expect the intelligence of youth to evolve to the wisdom of old age. The younger person is faster and sharper, and certainly, tests such as Raven's Matrices can show very large declines from age twenty to even fifty or sixty. Still, we place the older person in control of projects, organizations, countries. For management of complex systems, we take experience as the sine qua non.

Experience, of course, means increasing knowledge. In terms of the problem-solving programs we discussed in chapter 5, it means a richer long-term memory of important facts, relationships, and potential solutions. As problems are solved, the richer long-term memory gives more knowledge to work with.

An intriguing idea is that, as life is lived and knowledge is accumulated, the structure of that knowledge may itself depend on the intelligence that produced it—on the cognitive enclosures that were formed as problems were originally encountered and solved. Evidently, we do not store unstructured experience; we store the products of our own thoughts, our own interactions with our world. In chapter 5, I discussed the link between cognitive enclosure and abstraction. An abstract idea is something that applies across many individual cases. In other words, it expresses something constant across other, irrelevant variations. Justice is justice whether it holds in court or in a negotiation on the playground. Newton's laws hold whether the moving object is a train or a snowflake. In the cognitive enclosure that expresses an abstraction, essential features are retained, all else excluded.

With this reasoning we can see how the wisdom of age may indeed evolve, rather immediately and directly, from the intelligence of youth. A lifetime lived with clean, well-defined cognitive enclosures is a lifetime of learning, not just facts, but cleanly defined, useful facts. In domains in which we are expert, we do not just know a lot . . . the things that we know are apt fragments, apt abstractions, things that were useful many times before and that, when younger colleagues bring us new problems, are useful again. A good abstraction is always good; we can use it again and again across the multitude of life's variations.

We have barely begun on the neurophysiology of cognitive enclosures. On the lateral surface of the prefrontal cortex, we see many neurons coding the specific information of the current cognitive event. But how do the different parts of the multiple-demand system combine? What are their diverse roles? How do they interact in detail with other systems in the brain? How does the brain produce, not just one focused enclosure, but the whole program that runs a complex sequence of activity?

To answer these questions may require recordings, not just from single cells, but from many cells recorded simultaneously, in different parts of the multiple-demand system as well as elsewhere in the brain. How do neurons compare in diverse regions? How do they communicate with one another?

At this stage we have only speculations. Many kinds of information converge on the lateral prefrontal cortex, including neural descriptions of sights, sounds, touches, smells, material retrieved from long-term memory, information concerning goals and rewards. Here is a system optimally placed for assembling the many varied contents of different cognitive enclosures. As figure 6 (chapter 4) shows, however, multiple-demand activity also spreads downward from this region on the lateral surface of the brain, eventually disappearing into the deep fold that separates frontal from temporal lobes. Buried within this fold, activity extends into a structure, the anterior insula, with rather different connections. In our bodies are two parallel divisions of the nervous system. The skeletal nervous system controls the familiar movements of limbs, head, trunk, and so on. The autonomic system controls such bodily functions as heart rate and sweating. The insula has strong connections to the autonomic nervous system; it is concerned not just with the outside world but with the internal world of our own bodies.

Why should there be some intimate connection between mental demand and internal bodily function? We do not know, but on reflection, it is not so surprising. For many years we have known that mental challenges produce bodily reactions. A person who adds numbers in his or her head, or solves a problem in Raven's Matrices, will show a characteristic pattern of bodily changes: changes in the speed and regularity of the heartbeat, dilation of the pupils, sweating of the hands. There is some close link between bodily and mental effort—as we think, we do not just think, we strive. Is multiple-demand activity in the insula related to this aspect of thought—to the effort aspect?[12] If so, we might expect neurons there to be rather different from neurons of the lateral frontal surface. Their firing might relate not so much to information but more to demand.

Critical in any mental program is controlled transition from one step to the next. As we add a column of numbers, each number in turn must enter the focus of attention for addition to the current total. Then it must disappear, with only the new total carried forward as the eyes move to the next number in the column. In general, each step of a mental program produces results that later steps will need. The results must be carried forward as part of the input to the next enclosure; the operations that produced those results must terminate and disappear.

Here is a discovery from the laboratory of a father of prefrontal neurophysiology, Steven Wise.[13] For these experiments, the Wise group turned to the most forward tip of the prefrontal cortex, a region previously unexplored. As with all the best adventures, the discoveries were completely unexpected. In this task, the monkey went through a series of trials, one after the other. On each trial, a complex set of instructions told the monkey to make one of two eye movements: either to repeat the movement he had made on the previous trial or to change to the other. In many parts of the prefrontal cortex, the experimenters found what we know they should—neurons of many different kinds, coding many different aspects of the task. At the most forward tip, though, they found something quite new.

At the tip, neurons did not do many different things. In this task, instead, they followed one, remarkably consistent pattern. They fired at the end of each trial, at the moment the task was completed and the reward was received. And the only information they coded at this time was *which response the monkey had made*: the exact information that he would need to know when, on the next trial, he was instructed either to make the same movement again or to change it. These are the first results from a new part of the brain, and it is much too early to say exactly what they mean. Still, the results suggest activity just at the transition between one major division of the task and the next—activity coding nothing but the results to be carried forward, the results that will be needed at the next mental step.

Looking across brain systems, again, the critical question is integration. To assemble the contents of one cognitive enclosure and to move from one enclosure to the next, the components of the multiple-demand system must work, not just with one another, but with all manner of different brain systems. The right information must be gathered from the senses, the right knowledge retrieved from long-term memory, the right actions planned and executed. The complex, flexible neural code that we have seen in prefrontal neurons must be used. At present we know almost nothing of how this may be done.

There is a biggest, least answerable question of all. How far can human reason take us? Where are the limits?

The flexibility of the cognitive enclosure is something very different from the fixed innate releasing mechanism of the stickleback. It gives us spectacular power to conceive of objects, events, relationships, and abstractions from calculus to general relativity to the statistics of natural selection. The power is spectacular, but this does not mean that it is unlimited. As we seek for laws of the universe, we may remember that each law is also just a human idea. Potentially, it is shaped, not just by the universe it describes, but by the mind that conceives it.

To me it seems unlikely that our minds are constructed for unlimited conceptualization or understanding. A caterpillar lying along the blade of a leaf can apprehend just a few things—its position on the leaf, perhaps the angle of the sun that determines how it should orient its camouflaging markings, the position of the head to eat. A dog can conceive of much more, but it cannot imagine calculus. For every species on earth, comparison with ourselves tells us how limited is the power of its nervous system.

In this respect, is just one species different from all the others? Or is it rather that all of our human thoughts are by definition our own and that, just like the caterpillar, we can imagine only so far as our own nervous systems allow?

We do not know, and in a sense, we can never know. As we reason, we use our own reasoning machine. Surely it is a wonderful machine, taking us from the beginning to the end of time and from subatomic particles to the borders of the universe. Still, it is just another machine, constructed from many billions of nerve cells, like the caterpillar but more so. Perhaps we can never see beyond our own biological boundaries.

Notes

Prologue: The Cows in the River and the View toward the Malecón

1. K. Lorenz, *Studies in Animal and Human Behaviour*, vol. 1 (London: Methuen, 1970); N. Tinbergen, *The Study of Instinct* (Oxford: Clarendon Press, 1951).

2. A. Manning, *An Introduction to Animal Behaviour* (London: Edward Arnold, 1967).

3. J.-P. Ewert, "Neuroethology of Releasing Mechanisms: Prey-Catching in Toads," *Behavioral and Brain Sciences* (1987): 337–405.

4. Tinbergen, *Study of Instinct*.

Chapter 1: The Machine

1. J. R. Stroop, "Studies of Interference in Serial Verbal Reactions," *Journal of Experimental Psychology* (1935): 643–662.

2. D. E. Broadbent, *Perception and Communication* (London: Pergamon, 1958).

3. A. Treisman and G. Geffen, "Selective Attention: Perception or Response?" *Quarterly Journal of Experimental Psychology* (1967): 1–17.

4. A. M. Treisman, "Contextual Cues in Selective Listening," *Quarterly Journal of Experimental Psychology* (1960): 242–248.

5. P. C. Wason, "Problem Solving and Reasoning," *British Medical Bulletin* (1971): 206–210.

6. H. A. Simon, "A Behavioral Model of Rational Choice," *Quarterly Journal of Economics* (1955): 99–118.

7. S. Milgram, *Obedience to Authority: An Experimental View* (New York: Harper and Row, 1974).

8. A. G. Miller et al., "The Prediction and Perception of Obedience to Authority," *Journal of Personality* (1974): 23–42.

Chapter 2: A Regularity

1. C. Spearman, "General Intelligence, Objectively Determined and Measured," *American Journal of Psychology* (1904): 201–293.

2. Spearman, "General Intelligence, Objectively Determined and Measured," 277.

3. C. Spearman, *The Abilities of Man* (New York: Macmillan, 1927).

4. F. L. Schmidt and J. E. Hunter, "The Validity and Utility of Selection Methods in Personnel Psychology: Practical and Theoretical Implications of 85 Years of Research Findings," *Psychological Bulletin* (1998): 262–274.

5. A. R. Jensen, *The g Factor* (Westport, CT: Praeger, 1998).

6. J. C. Raven, J. H. Court, and J. Raven, *Manual for Raven's Progressive Matrices and Vocabulary Scales* (London: H. K. Lewis, 1988).

7. J. D. Schall, "Neural Correlates of Decision Processes: Neural and Mental Chronometry," *Current Opinion in Neurobiology* (2003): 182–186.

8. Spearman, "General Intelligence, Objectively Determined and Measured," 273.

9. J. B. Carroll, *Human Cognitive Abilities: A Survey of Factor-Analytic Studies* (New York: Cambridge University Press, 1993).

10. R. B. Cattell, *Abilities: Their Structure, Growth and Action* (Boston: Houghton-Mifflin, 1971).

11. M. Sherif and C. W. Sherif, *Social Psychology* (New York: Harper and Row, 1969).

12. L. J. Kamin, *The Science and Politics of I.Q.* (Potomac, MD: Erlbaum, 1974).

Chapter 3: Inside

1. J.-P. Ewert, "Neuroethology of Releasing Mechanisms: Prey-Catching in Toads," *Behavioral and Brain Sciences* (1987): 337–405.

2. E. R. Kandel, *In Search of Memory: The Emergence of a New Science of Mind* (New York: W. W. Norton, 2006).

3. J. Moran and R. Desimone, "Selective Attention Gates Visual Processing in the Extrastriate Cortex," *Science* (1985): 782–784.

4. A. D. Milner and M. A. Goodale, *The Visual Brain in Action* (Oxford: Oxford University Press, 1995).

5. R. McGlinchey-Berroth, "Visual Information Processing in Hemispatial Neglect," *Trends in Cognitive Sciences* (1997): 91–97.

6. H. H. J. Op de Beeck, J. Haushofer, and N. Kanwisher, "Interpreting fMRI Data: Maps, Modules, and Dimensions," *Nature Reviews Neuroscience* (2008): 123–135.

7. D. E. Broadbent, *Perception and Communication* (London: Pergamon, 1958).

8. A. M. Treisman and A. Davies, "Divided Attention to Ear and Eye," in *Attention and Performance IV*, ed. S. Kornblum (London: Academic, 1973), 101–117.

Chapter 4: Making the Link

1. G. H. Thomson, *The Factorial Analysis of Human Ability*, 5th ed. (London: University of London Press, 1951).

2. J. R. Hodges et al., "Semantic Dementia: Progressive Fluent Aphasia with Temporal Lobe Atrophy," *Brain* (1992): 1783–1806.

3. D. Kahneman, R. Ben-Ishai, and M. Lotan, "Relation of a Test of Attention to Road Accidents," *Journal of Applied Psychology* (1973): 113–115.

4. A. R. Luria, *Higher Cortical Functions in Man* (London: Tavistock, 1966).

5. B. Milner, "Effects of Different Brain Lesions on Card Sorting," *Archives of Neurology* (1963): 90–100.

6. L. Bianchi, *The Mechanism of the Brain and the Function of the Frontal Lobes* (Edinburgh: Livingstone, 1922), 184.

7. W. Penfield and J. Evans, "The Frontal Lobe in Man: A Clinical Study of Maximum Removals," *Brain* (1935): 115–133.

8. Penfield and Evans, "Frontal Lobe in Man," 130–131.

9. Penfield and Evans, "Frontal Lobe in Man," 131.

10. Luria, *Higher Cortical Functions in Man*, 245, 249.

11. Luria, *Higher Cortical Functions in Man*, 268.

12. Luria, *Higher Cortical Functions in Man*, 248–249.

13. D. O. Hebb and W. Penfield, "Human Behavior after Extensive Removal from the Frontal Lobes," *Archives of Neurology and Psychiatry* (1940): 421–438.

14. S. Weinstein and H. L. Teuber, "Effects of Penetrating Brain Injury on Intelligence Test Scores," *Science* (1957): 1036–1037.

15. H. L. Teuber, "Unity and Diversity of Frontal Lobe Functions," *Acta Neurobiologiae Experimentalis* (1972): 615–656, quotation on 638.

16. J. Duncan, P. Burgess, and H. Emslie, "Fluid Intelligence after Frontal Lobe Lesions," *Neuropsychologia* (1995): 261–268.

17. J. Duncan and A. M. Owen, "Common Regions of the Human Frontal Lobe Recruited by Diverse Cognitive Demands," *Trends in Neurosciences* (2000): 475–483.

18. J. Duncan, "Brain Mechanisms of Attention," *Quarterly Journal of Experimental Psychology* (2006): 2–27.

19. J. Duncan et al., "A Neural Basis for General Intelligence," *Science* (2000): 457–460; V. Prabhakaran et al., "Neural Substrates of Fluid Reasoning: An fMRI Study of Neocortical Activation during Performance of the Raven's Progressive Matrices Test," *Cognitive Psychology* (1997): 43–63; S. J. Bishop et al., "COMT val158met Genotype Affects Recruitment of Neural Mechanisms Supporting Fluid Intelligence," *Cerebral Cortex* (2008): 2132–2140.

20. P. A. Carpenter, M. A. Just, and P. Shell, "What One Intelligence

Test Measures: A Theoretical Account of the Processing in the Raven Progressive Matrices Test," *Psychological Review* (1990): 404–431.

21. J. Duncan et al., "Intelligence and the Frontal Lobe: The Organization of Goal-Directed Behavior," *Cognitive Psychology* (1996): 257–303.

22. L. H. Phillips and J. D. Henry, "An Evaluation of the Frontal Lobe Theory of Cognitive Aging," in *Measuring the Mind: Speed, Control, and Age*, ed. J. Duncan, L. H. Phillips, and P. McLeod (Oxford: Oxford University Press, 2005), 191–216.

23. T. C. Neylan, "Frontal Lobe Function: Mr. Phineas Gage's Famous Injury," *Journal of Neuropsychiatry and Clinical Neurosciences* (1999): 280–281, quotation on 280; J. M. Harlow, "Passage of an Iron Rod through the Head" [1848], *Journal of Neuropsychiatry and Clinical Neurosciences* (1999): 281–283; H. Damasio et al., "The Return of Phineas Gage: Clues about the Brain from the Skull of a Famous Patient," *Science* (1994): 1102–1105.

24. J. D. Steele and S. M. Lawrie, "Segregation of Cognitive and Emotional Function in the Prefrontal Cortex: A Stereotactic Meta-Analysis," *Neuroimage* (2004): 868–875.

25. Teuber, *Unity and Diversity of Frontal Lobe Functions*, 637.

Chapter 5: The Demystification of Thought

1. A. Newell, J. C. Shaw, and H. A. Simon, "The Processes of Creative Thinking," in *Contemporary Approaches to Creative Thinking*, ed. H. E. Gruber, G. Terrell, and M. Wertheimer (New York: Atherton, 1962), 63–119.

2. A. Newell, J. C. Shaw, and H. A. Simon, "Elements of a Theory of Human Problem Solving," *Psychological Review* (1958): 151–166, quotation on 152.

3. A. Newell, *Unified Theories of Cognition* (Cambridge, MA: Harvard University Press, 1990); J. R. Anderson and C. Lebiere, *The Atomic Components of Thought* (Mahwah, NJ: Erlbaum, 1998).

4. G. A. Miller, E. Galanter, and K. H. Pribram, *Plans and the Structure of Behavior* (New York: Holt, Rinehart and Winston, 1960).

5. E. Tulving, "Episodic and Semantic Memory," in *Organization of*

Memory, ed. E. Tulving and W. Donaldson (New York: Academic, 1972), 381–403.

6. A. Newell and H. A. Simon, *Human Problem Solving* (Englewood Cliffs, NJ: Prentice-Hall, 1972).

7. B. Hayes-Roth and F. Hayes-Roth, "A Cognitive Model of Planning," *Cognitive Science* (1979): 275–310.

8. Newell, Shaw, and Simon, "Elements of a Theory of Human Problem Solving," 152.

9. E. D. Sacerdoti, "Planning in a Hierarchy of Abstraction Spaces," *Artificial Intelligence* (1974): 115–135.

10. W. Köhler, *The Mentality of Apes* (London: Kegan Paul Trench Trübner, 1925).

11. Köhler, *Mentality of Apes*, 42–43.

12. N. R. F. Maier, "Reasoning in Humans: II. The Solution of a Problem and Its Appearance in Consciousness," *Journal of Comparative Psychology* (1931): 181–194.

13. C. A. Kaplan and H. A. Simon, "In Search of Insight," *Cognitive Psychology* (1990): 374–419.

14. K. Duncker, "On Problem Solving," *Psychological Monographs* (1945): 1–113.

15. D. Y. Kimberg and M. J. Farah, "A Unified Account of Cognitive Impairments Following Frontal Lobe Damage: The Role of Working Memory in Complex, Organized Behavior," *Journal of Experimental Psychology: General* (1993): 411–428.

Chapter 6: Up Close

1. J. Müller, *Zur Vergleichenden Physiologie des Gesichtssinnes des Menschen und der Tiere* (Leipzig: C. Knobloch, 1826).

2. C. F. Jacobsen, "Functions of Frontal Association Area in Primates," *Archives of Neurology and Psychiatry* (1935): 558–569.

3. J. M. Fuster and G. E. Alexander, "Neuron Activity Related to Short-Term Memory," *Science* (1971): 652–654.

4. E. V. Evarts, "Pyramidal Tract Activity Associated with a Conditioned Hand Movement in the Monkey," *Journal of Neurophysiology* (1966): 1011–1027.

5. S. Funahashi, C. J. Bruce, and P. S. Goldman-Rakic, "Mnemonic Coding of Visual Space in the Monkey's Dorsolateral Prefrontal Cortex," *Journal of Neurophysiology* (1989): 331–349.

6. L. G. Ungerleider and M. Mishkin, "Two Cortical Visual Systems," in *Analysis of Visual Behavior*, ed. D. J. Ingle, M. A. Goodale, and R. J. W. Mansfield (Cambridge, MA: MIT Press, 1982), 549–586.

7. P. Goldman-Rakic, "Topography of Cognition: Parallel Distributed Networks in Primate Association Cortex," *Annual Review of Neuroscience* (1988): 137–156; F. A. W. Wilson, S. P. Scalaidhe, and P. S. Goldman-Rakic, "Dissociation of Object and Spatial Processing Domains in Primate Prefrontal Cortex," *Science* (1993): 1955–1958.

8. J. M. Fuster, *The Prefrontal Cortex: Anatomy, Physiology, and Neuropsychology of the Frontal Lobe*, 2nd ed. (New York: Raven, 1989).

9. S. C. Rao, G. Rainer, and E. K. Miller, "Integration of What and Where in the Primate Prefrontal Cortex," *Science* (1997): 821–824.

10. J. Duncan, "An Adaptive Coding Model of Neural Function in Prefrontal Cortex," *Nature Reviews Neuroscience* (2001): 820–829.

11. D. J. Freedman et al., "Categorical Representation of Visual Stimuli in the Primate Prefrontal Cortex," *Science* (2001): 312–316.

12. A. Nieder, D. J. Freedman, and E. K. Miller, "Representation of the Quantity of Visual Items in the Primate Prefrontal Cortex," *Science* (2002): 1708–1711.

13. E. Procyk, Y. L. Tanaka, and J. P. Joseph, "Anterior Cingulate Activity during Routine and Non-Routine Sequential Behaviors in Macaques," *Nature Neuroscience* (2000): 502–508.

14. U. Neisser and R. Becklen, "Selective Looking: Attending to Visually Specified Events," *Cognitive Psychology* (1975): 480–494.

15. J. Moran and R. Desimone, "Selective Attention Gates Visual Processing in the Extrastriate Cortex," *Science* (1985): 782–784.

16. J. H. Reynolds, L. Chelazzi, and R. Desimone, "Competitive

Mechanisms Subserve Attention in Macaque Areas V2 and V4," *Journal of Neuroscience* (1999): 1736–1743.

17. J. Duncan, "Selective Attention and the Organization of Visual Information," *Journal of Experimental Psychology: General* (1984): 501–517; K. M. O'Craven, P. E. Downing, and N. Kanwisher, "fMRI Evidence for Objects as the Units of Attentional Selection," *Nature* (1999): 584–587.

18. D. J. Freedman et al., "Stimulus-Specificity of Category-Related Neurons in the Monkey Prefrontal Cortex (PFC) and Inferior Temporal Cortex (ITC). Program No. 160.12. Abstract Viewer/Itinerary Planner." Washington, DC: Society for Neuroscience, 2002.

19. M. Kusunoki et al., "Detection of Fixed and Variable Targets in the Monkey Prefrontal Cortex," *Cerebral Cortex* (2009): 2535–2547.

20. N. Sigala et al., "Hierarchical Coding for Sequential Task Events in the Monkey Prefrontal Cortex," *Proceedings of the National Academy of Sciences USA* (2008): 11969–11974.

21. M. Rigotti et al., "The Importance of Neural Diversity in Complex Cognitive Tasks. Program No. 929.3. Abstract Viewer/Itinerary Planner." Washington, DC: Society for Neuroscience, 2007.

22. P. O'Brian, *HMS Surprise* (London: W. W. Norton, 1991), 289.

23. O'Brian, *HMS Surprise*, 290.

Chapter 7: The Box

1. N. Z. Kirkham, L. Cruess, and A. Diamond, "Helping Children Apply Their Knowledge to Their Behavior on a Dimension-Switching Task," *Developmental Science* (2003): 449–476.

2. B. M. Hood, "Gravity Rules for 2- to 4-Year Olds?" *Cognitive Development* (1995): 577–598.

3. D. Kahneman, "A Perspective on Judgment and Choice: Mapping Bounded Rationality," *American Psychologist* (2003): 697–720.

4. B. J. McNeil et al., "On the Elicitation of Preferences for Alternative Therapies," *New England Journal of Medicine* (1982): 1259–1262.

5. Kahneman, "Perspective on Judgment and Choice."

6. Kahneman, "Perspective on Judgment and Choice," 709.

7. P. Slovic et al., "Rational Actors or Rational Fools: Implications of the Affect Heuristic for Behavioral Economics," *Journal of Socio-Economics* (2002): 329–342; A. Tversky and D. Kahneman, "The Framing of Decisions and the Psychology of Choice," *Science* (1981): 453–458.

8. E. Shafir, I. Simonson, and A. Tversky, "Reason-Based Choice," *Cognition* (1993): 11–36.

9. W. H. Desvouges et al., "Measuring Natural Resource Damages with Contingent Valuation: Tests of Validity and Reliability," in *Contingent Valuation: A Critical Assessment*, ed. J. A. Hausman (Amsterdam: North-Holland, 1993), 91–159; G. F. Loewenstein et al., "Risk as Feelings," *Psychological Bulletin* (2001): 267–286.

10. L. Festinger, *A Theory of Cognitive Dissonance* (Stanford, CA: Stanford University Press, 1957).

11. J. W. Brehm, "Postdecision Changes in the Desirability of Alternatives," *Journal of Abnormal and Social Psychology* (1956): 384–389.

12. E. Aronson and J. Mills, "The Effect of Severity of Initiation on Liking for a Group," *Journal of Abnormal and Social Psychology* (1959): 177–181.

13. C. G. Lord, L. Ross, and M. R. Lepper, "Biased Assimilation and Attitude Polarization: The Effects of Prior Theories on Subsequently Considered Evidence," *Journal of Personality and Social Psychology* (1979): 2098–2109, quotation on 2099.

14. D. Frey and M. Rosch, "Information Seeking after Decisions: The Roles of Novelty of Information and Decision Reversibility," *Personality and Social Psychology Bulletin* (1984): 91–98.

15. Slovic et al., "Rational Actors or Rational Fools."

16. J. D. Teasdale, "Cognitive Vulnerability to Persistent Depression," *Cognition and Emotion* (1988): 247–274.

17. E. J. Johnson et al., "Framing, Probability Distortions, and Insurance Decisions," *Journal of Risk and Uncertainty* (1993): 35–51.

18. A. H. Mokdad et al., "Actual Causes of Death in the United States, 2000," *Journal of the American Medical Association* (2004): 1238–1245.

19. M. Sherif and C. W. Sherif, *Social Psychology* (New York: Harper and Row, 1969).

20. F. Bacon, *The New Organon and Related Writings* [1620] (New York: Liberal Arts Press, 1960), 50.

21. G. M. Gilbert, *Nuremberg Diary* (New York: Signet, 1947), 278–279.

22. L. Mann and I. L. Janis, "A Follow-up Study on the Long-Term Effects of Emotional Role Playing," *Journal of Personality and Social Psychology* (1968): 657–671; E. H. Schein, "The Chinese Indoctrination Program for Prisoners of War: A Study of Attempted Brainwashing," *Psychiatry* (1956): 149–172.

23. N. Schwarz and G. L. Clore, "Mood, Misattribution, and Judgments of Well-Being: Informative and Directive Functions of Affective States," *Journal of Personality and Social Psychology* (1983): 513–523; Kahneman, "Perspective on Judgment and Choice."

24. D. Kahneman et al., "Would You Be Happier If You Were Richer? A Focusing Illusion," *Science* (2006): 1908–1910; C. Nickerson et al., "Zeroing in on the Dark Side of the American Dream: A Closer Look at the Negative Consequences of the Goal for Financial Success," *Psychological Science* (2003): 531–536.

Chapter 8: The One Sure Thing

1. J. Duncan et al., "Goal Neglect and Spearman's g: Competing Parts of a Complex Task," *Journal of Experimental Psychology: General* (2008): 131–148.

2. J. D. Haynes and G. Rees, "Decoding Mental States from Brain Activity in Humans," *Nature Reviews Neuroscience* (2006): 523–534.

3. M. Stokes et al., "Top-Down Activation of Shape-Specific Population Codes in Visual Cortex During Mental Imagery," *Journal of Neuroscience* (2009): 1565–1572.

4. J. D. Haynes et al., "Reading Hidden Intentions in the Human Brain," *Current Biology* (2007): 323–328.

5. D. Norman and T. Shallice, *Attention to Action: Willed and Automatic*

Control of Behavior, Report no. 8006 (San Diego: University of California, Center for Human Information Processing, 1980).

6. P. M. Fitts and M. I. Posner, *Human Performance* (Belmont, CA: Brooks/ Cole, 1967); P. McLeod, P. Sommerville, and N. Reed, "Are Automated Actions beyond Conscious Access?" in *Measuring the Mind: Speed, Control, and Age*, ed. J. Duncan, L. H. Phillips, and P. McLeod (Oxford: Oxford University Press, 2005), 359–372.

7. J. Duncan and A. M. Owen, "Common Regions of the Human Frontal Lobe Recruited by Diverse Cognitive Demands," *Trends in Neurosciences* (2000): 475–483.

8. P. L. Ackerman, "Determinants of Individual Differences during Skill Acquisition: Cognitive Abilities and Information Processing," *Journal of Experimental Psychology: General* (1988): 288–318.

9. S. Everling et al., "Selective Representation of Task-Relevant Objects and Locations in the Monkey Prefrontal Cortex," *European Journal of Neuroscience* (2006): 2197–2214.

10. P. J. Olesen, H. Westerberg, and T. Klingberg, "Increased Prefrontal and Parietal Activity after Training of Working Memory," *Nature Neuroscience* (2004): 75–79; S. M. Jaeggi et al., "Improving Fluid Intelligence with Training on Working Memory," *Proceedings of the National Academy of Sciences USA* (2008): 6829–6833.

11. R. Plomin and Y. Kovas, "Generalist Genes and Learning Disabilities," *Pyschological Bulletin* (2005): 592–617.

12. H. D. Critchley et al., "Neural Activity Relating to Generation and Representation of Galvanic Skin Conductance Response: A Functional Magnetic Resonance Imaging Study," *Journal of Neuroscience* (2000): 3033–3040.

13. S. Tsujimoto, A. Genovesio, and S. P. Wise, "The Neurophysiology of Frontal Pole Cortex in Rhesus Monkeys. Program No. 388.2. Abstract Viewer/Itinerary Planner." Washington, DC: Society for Neuroscience, 2008.

Index

The *Abilities of Man* (Spearman), 37,
43
abstraction, 140–142, 219
academic ability, 30, 32, 44
active control and organization.
See Goal-directed action
active inhibition, 154
aging, 47–48, 111
Alexander, Garrett, 156–157
American Journal of Psychology and
Spearman, 29–30
amnesia, 66, 76
anterior insula, 220, 221
aphasias, 66. *See also* Language
Army General Classification Test,
97–98
artificial intelligence, 118–134, 145–
146
attention: and cognitive enclosures,
168–169; and frontal lobes, 171;
and *g* factor, 43; limits of, 15–17,
71; and practiced tasks, 214; as

sensory input filter, 169. *See also*
Selective attention
auditory information: and cerebral
cortex, 65; and consciousness,
148; and selective attention, 16–
17, 71, 168
authority and social bias, 21
autonomic nervous system, 220–221
axons, 59

Bacon, Francis, 13, 197
Bianchi, Leonardo, 88
bias: coherence, 190–195; confirmation, 19; consistency, 190–195,
202–203; social, 21, 195–196
Binet, Alfred, 36–37, 100
Blair, Tony, 198–199
bonds, 74–75
bounded rationality, 20
brain anatomy and function, 55–72;
divide-and-conquer strategy for
studying, 65–70, 111–112, 113;